GHOST STORIES

Cursed Creatures

GARETH**STEVENS**

GS PUBLISHING

A Member of the WRC Media Family of Companies

Please visit our web site at: **www.garethstevens.com**
For a free color catalog describing Gareth Stevens Publishing's
list of high-quality books and multimedia programs, call
1-800-542-2595 (USA) or 1-800-387-3178 (Canada).
Gareth Stevens Publishing's fax: (414) 332-3567.

Library of Congress Cataloging-in-Publication Data

Cursed creatures.
     v. cm. — (Ghost stories)
   ISBN-10: 0-8368-6821-8 — ISBN-13: 978-0-8368-6821-0 (lib. bdg.)
    1. Children's stories. 2. Horror tales. [1. Short stories.
  2. Horror stories.] I. Series.
 PZ5.C938   2006
 [Fic]—dc22   2006012442

This North American edition first published in 2007 by
Gareth Stevens Publishing
A Member of the WRC Media Family of Companies
330 West Olive Street, Suite 100
Milwaukee, WI 53212 USA

This U.S. edition copyright © 2007 by Gareth Stevens, Inc.
Original edition copyright © 2005 by Miles Kelly Publishing Ltd.
First published in Great Britain in 2005 by Bardfield Press,
Bardfield Centre, Great Bardfield, Essex, CM7 4SL, United Kingdom.

Series editorial director: Belinda Gallagher
Series art director: Jo Brewer
Series assistant editors: Rosalind McGuire and Hannah Todd
Series designer: Tom Slemmings
Series picture research manager: Liberty Newton
Series picture researcher: Laura Faulder
Series production: Estela Boulton and Elizabeth Brunwin
Series scanning and reprographics: Anthony Cambray, Mike Coupe, and Ian Paulyn
Introduction ("Cursed Creatures"): Vic Parker

Gareth Stevens editorial direction: Mark J. Sachner
Gareth Stevens editor: Tea Benduhn
Gareth Stevens art direction and design: Tammy West
Gareth Stevens art design: Scott Krall and Kami Strunsee
Gareth Stevens production: Jessica Morris and Robert Kraus

Artwork and photographic credits: Martin Angel, Vanessa Card, Castrol, CMCD, CORBIS,
Corel digitalSTOCK, Jon Davis/Linden Artists, Peter Dennis/Linda Rogers Associates, digitalvision,
Flat Earth, John Foxx, Hemera, Richard Hook/Linden Artists, ILN, PhotoAlto, PhotoDisc, PhotoEssentials,
PhotoPro, Eric Rowe/Linden Artists, Mike Saunders, StockbyteColin Sullivan/Beehive Illustration,
Gwen Tourret/B. L. Kearley, Rudi Vizi, Mike White/Temple Rogers. All other artworks are from
the Miles Kelly Artwork Bank.

Printed in the United States of America

1 2 3 4 5 6 7 8 9 10 09 08 07 06

TABLE OF CONTENTS

Cursed Creatures

THERE ARE MANY THINGS OTHER THAN GHOSTS

THAT GO BUMP IN THE NIGHT. HERE ARE TALES OF VAMPIRES

AND MUMMIES, NAMELESS MONSTERS, AND PHANTOM BEASTS,

EVIL ALTER EGOS AND SCRAPS OF CORPSES BROUGHT BACK TO LIFE.

WELCOME TO THE WORLD OF THE UNDEAD.

Cursed Creatures is filled with creepy stories to chill you, thrill you, and send shivers down your spine. Here are some of the very best from a rich tradition of terrifying tales that dates back to Christmas Eve, 1764. It was then that the first ever "horror" novel was published, *The Castle of Otranto*, by Horace Walpole. His was an eerie tale of ghosts, family curses, and macabre goings-on, set in a foreign land during medieval times – an era when everyone believed in the supernatural and many superstitions made them fearful. *The Castle of Otranto* captivated the imagination of eighteenth-century readers who demanded more eerie tales.

Through the Victorian era (1837–1901), families and friends loved to gather around the parlor fire on dark evenings to listen to sinister and spooky stories. Spiritualism also became fashionable, and many Victorians dabbled in attempts to contact the dead. Victorian authors transformed Gothic horror-writing by developing it in exciting directions. They did away with remote locations and past times and brought horrors right to their readers' front doors.

In 1918, Virginia Woolf wrote an article for the *Times Literary Supplement* exploring the reasons that ghost stories are so irresistible. She decided that "It is pleasant to be afraid when we are conscious that we are in no kind of danger."

So settle back and enjoy these haunting tales, safe in the knowledge that there's no such thing as a ghost... or is there?

WHAT WAS IT?

Fitz-James O'Brien

Extract

It was the tenth of July. After dinner was over I repaired with my friend, Dr. Hammond, to the garden to smoke my evening pipe. The Doctor and myself found ourselves in an unusually metaphysical mood. We lit our large meerschaums, filled with fine Turkish tobacco; we paced to and fro, conversing. A strange perversity dominated the currents of our thoughts. They would *not* flow through the sunlit channels into which we strove to divert them. For some unaccountable reason they constantly diverged into dark and lonesome beds, where a continual gloom brooded. It was in vain that, after our old fashion, we flung ourselves on the shores of the East, and talked of its gay bazaars, of the splendors of the time of Haroun, of harems and golden palaces. Black genies continually arose from the depths of our talk, and expanded, like the one the fisherman released from the copper vessel, until they blotted everything bright from

6

our vision. Insensibly, we yielded to the occult force that swayed us, and indulged in gloomy speculation. We had talked some time upon the proneness of the human mind to mysticism and the almost universal love of the Terrible, when Hammond suddenly said to me, "What do you consider to be the greatest element of terror?"

The question, I own, puzzled me. That many things were terrible, I knew. Stumbling over a corpse in the dark; beholding, as I once did, a woman floating down a deep and rapid river, with wildly lifted arms and awful upturned face, uttering as she sank, shrieks that rent one's heart, while we, the spectators, stood frozen at a window which overhung the river at a height of sixty feet, unable to make the slightest effort to save her, but dumbly watching her last supreme agony and her disappearance. A shattered wreck, with no life visible, encountered floating listlessly on the ocean, is a terrible object, for it suggests a huge terror, the proportions of which are veiled. But it now struck me for the first time that there must be one great and ruling embodiment of fear – a 'king of terrors' to which all others must succumb. What might it be? To what train of circumstances would it owe its existence?

"I confess, Hammond," I replied to my friend, "I never considered the subject before. That there must be something more terrible than any other thing, I feel. I cannot attempt, however, even the most vague definition."

"I am somewhat like you, Harry," he answered. "I feel my capacity to experience a terror greater than anything yet

conceived by the human mind – something combining
in fearful and unnatural amalgamation hitherto supposed
incompatible elements. The calling of the voices in Brockden
Brown's novel of *Wieland* is awful; so is the picture of the
Dweller of the Threshold, in Bulwer's *Zanoni*; but," he added,
shaking his head gloomily, "there is something more horrible
still than these."

"Look here, Hammond," I rejoined, "let us drop this kind
of talk, for heaven's sake!"

"I don't know what's the matter with me tonight," he
replied, "but my brain is running upon all sorts of weird and
awful thoughts. I feel as if I could write a story like Hoffman
tonight, if I were only master of a literary style."

"Well, if we are going to be Hoffmanesque in our talk,
I'm off to bed. How sultry it is! Goodnight, Hammond."

"Goodnight, Harry. Pleasant dreams to you."

"To you, gloomy wretch, genies, ghouls, and enchanters."

We parted, and each sought his respective chamber.
I undressed quickly and got into bed, taking with me, according
to my usual custom, a book, over which I generally read myself
to sleep. I opened the volume as soon as I had laid my head
upon the pillow, and instantly flung it to the other side of the
room. It was Goudon's *History of Monsters* – a curious French
work which I had lately imported from Paris, but which, in the
state of mind I had then reached, was anything but an agreeable
companion. I resolved to go to sleep at once so, turning down
my gas until nothing but a little blue point of light glimmered
on the top of the tube, I composed myself to rest.

The room was in total darkness. The atom of gas that still remained lighted did not illuminate a distance of three inches round the burner. I desperately drew my arm across my eyes as if to shut out even the darkness, and tried to think of nothing. It was in vain. The confounded themes touched on by Hammond in the garden kept obtruding themselves on my brain. I battled against them. I erected ramparts of would-be blankness of intellect to keep them out. They still crowded upon me. While I was lying still as a corpse, hoping that by a perfect physical inaction I should hasten mental repose, an awful incident occurred. Something dropped, as it seemed, from the ceiling, plumb upon my chest, and I felt two bony hands encircling my throat, endeavoring to choke me.

I am no coward, and am possessed of considerable physical strength. The suddenness of the attack, instead of stunning me, strung every nerve to its highest tension. My body acted from instinct, before my brain had time to realize the terrors of my position. In an instant, I wound two muscular arms around the creature and squeezed it, with all the strength of despair, against my chest. In a few seconds the bony hands that had fastened on my throat loosened their hold, and I was free to breathe once more. Then commenced a struggle of awful intensity. Immersed in the most profound darkness, totally ignorant of the nature of the thing by which I was so suddenly attacked, finding my grasp slipping every moment (by reason, it seemed to me, of the entire nakedness of my assailant) bitten with sharp teeth in the shoulder, neck and chest, having every moment to protect my throat against

9

a pair of sinewy, agile hands, which my utmost efforts could not confine – these were a combination of circumstances to combat which required all the strength, skill, and courage that I possessed.

At last, after a silent, deadly, exhausting struggle, I got my assailant under by a series of incredible efforts of strength. Once pinned, with my knee on what I made out to be its chest, I knew that I was victor. I rested for a moment to breathe. I heard the creature beneath me panting in the darkness, and felt the violent throbbing of a heart. It was apparently as exhausted as I was – that was one comfort. At this moment I remembered that I usually placed under my pillow, before going to bed, a large yellow silk pocket handkerchief, for use during the night. I felt for it instantly; it was there. In a few seconds more I had, after a fashion, pinioned the creature's arms.

I now felt tolerably secure. There was nothing more to be done but to turn on the gas and, having first seen what my midnight assailant was like, arouse the household. I will confess to being actuated by a certain pride in not giving the alarm before; I wished to make the capture alone and unaided.

Never losing my hold for an instant, I slipped from the bed to the floor, dragging my captive with me. I had but a few steps to make to reach the gas burner and these I made with the greatest caution, holding the creature in a grip like a vice. At last I got within arm's length of the tiny speck of blue light which told me where the gas burner lay. Quick as lightning I released my grasp with one hand and let on the full flood of light. Then I turned to look at my captive.

I cannot even attempt to give any definition of my sensations the instant after I turned on the gas. I suppose I must have shrieked with terror, for in less than a minute afterward my room was crowded with the inmates of the house. I shudder now as I think of that awful moment. I saw nothing! I had one arm firmly clasped round a breathing, panting, corporeal shape, my other hand gripped with all its strength a throat as warm, and apparently fleshly, as my own; and yet, with this living substance in my grasp, with its body pressed against my own, and all in the bright glare of a large jet of gas, I absolutely beheld nothing! Not even an outline – a vapor!

I do not, even at this hour, realize the situation in which I found myself. I cannot recall the astounding incident thoroughly. Imagination in vain tries to compass the awful paradox.

It breathed. I felt its warm breath upon my cheek. It struggled fiercely. It had hands. They clutched me. Its skin was smooth, like my own. There it lay, pressed close up against me, solid as stone – and yet utterly invisible!

I wonder that I did not faint or go mad on the instant. Some wonderful instinct must have sustained me; for, absolutely, in place of loosening my hold on the terrible enigma, I seemed to gain an additional strength in my moment of horror, and tightened my grasp with such wonderful force that I felt the creature shivering with agony.

Just then Hammond entered my room at the head of the household. As soon as he beheld my face – which, I suppose, must have been an awful sight to look at – he hastened forward, crying, "Great heaven, Harry! What has happened?"

"Hammond! Hammond!" I cried, "Come here. Oh! This is awful! I have been attacked in bed by something or other, which I have hold of; but I can't see it. I can't see it!"

Hammond, doubtless struck by the unfeigned horror expressed in my countenance, made one or two steps forward with an anxious, yet puzzled, expression. A very audible titter burst from the remainder of my visitors. This suppressed laughter made me furious. To laugh at a human being in my position! It was the worst species of cruelty. Now, I can understand why the appearance of a man struggling violently, as it would seem, with an airy nothing and calling for assistance against a vision, should have appeared ludicrous. Then, so great was my rage against the mocking crowd that had I the power, I would have stricken them dead where they stood.

"Hammond! Hammond!" I cried again, despairingly. "For God's sake come to me. I can hold the – the Thing but a short while longer. It is overpowering me. Help me! Help me!"

"Harry," whispered Hammond, approaching me, "stop fooling about."

"I swear to you, Hammond, that this is no joke," I answered, in the same low tone. "Don't you see how it shakes my whole frame with its struggles? If you don't believe me, convince yourself. Feel it – touch it."

Hammond advanced and laid his hand on the spot I indicated. A wild cry of horror burst from him. He had felt it!

In a moment he had discovered somewhere in my room a long piece of cord, and was the next instant winding it and knotting it about the body of the unseen being that I clasped in my arms.

"Harry," he said, in a hoarse, agitated voice, for, though he preserved his presence of mind, he was deeply moved, "Harry, it's all safe now. You may let go, old fellow, if you're tired. The Thing can't move."

I was utterly exhausted, and I gladly loosed my hold.

Hammond stood holding the ends of the cord that bound the invisible thing, twisted round his hand, while before him, self-supporting as it were, he beheld a rope laced and interlaced, and stretching tightly round a vacant space. I never saw a man look so thoroughly stricken with awe. Nevertheless his face expressed all the courage and determination which I knew him to possess. His lips, although white, were set firmly, and one could perceive

13

at a glance that, although stricken with fear, he was
not daunted.

The confusion that ensued among the guests of the house
who were witnesses of this extraordinary scene between
Hammond and myself – who beheld the pantomime of binding
this struggling something – who beheld me almost sinking from
physical exhaustion when my task of jailer was over – the
confusion and terror that took possession of the bystanders,
when they saw all this, was beyond description. The weaker
ones fled from the apartment. The few who remained clustered
near the door. Still incredulity broke out through their terror.
They had not the courage to satisfy themselves, and yet they
doubted. They were incredulous. How could a solid, breathing
body be invisible, they asked. My reply was this. I gave a sign
to Hammond, and both of us – conquering our fearful
repugnance to touch the invisible creature – lifted it from
the ground, manacled as it was, and took it to my bed.

"Now, my friends," I said, as Hammond and myself
held the creature suspended over the bed, "I can give
you self-evident proof that here is a solid, ponderable
body which, nevertheless, you cannot see. Be good
enough to watch the surface of the bed attentively."

I was astonished at my own courage in treating this
strange event so calmly; but I had recovered from my first
terror, and felt a sort of scientific pride in the affair which
dominated every other feeling.

The eyes of the bystanders were immediately fixed on my
bed. At a given signal, Hammond and I let the creature fall.

There was the dull sound of a heavy body alighting on a soft mass. The timbers of the bed creaked. A deep impression marked itself distinctly on the pillow, and on the bed itself. The crowd who witnessed this gave a low, universal cry and rushed from the room. Hammond and I were left alone.

We remained silent for some time, listening to the low, irregular breathing of the creature on the bed, and watching the rustle of the bedclothes as it impotently struggled to free itself from confinement. Then Hammond spoke.

"Harry, this is awful."

"Aye, awful."

"But not unaccountable."

"Not unaccountable! What do you mean? Such a thing has never occurred since the birth of the world. God grant that I am not mad, and that this is not an insane fantasy!"

"Let us reason a little, Harry. Here is a solid body which we touch, but which we cannot see. The fact is so unusual that it strikes us with terror. Is there no parallel, though, for such a phenomenon? Take a piece of pure glass. It is tangible and transparent. A certain chemical coarseness is all that prevents its being so entirely transparent as to be totally invisible. It is not theoretically impossible to make a glass which shall not reflect a single ray of light – a glass so pure and homogeneous in its atoms that the rays from the sun shall pass through it. We do not see the air, and yet we feel it."

"That's all very well Hammond, but these are inanimate substances. Glass does not breathe, air does not breathe. This thing has a heart that palpitates – a will that moves it."

"You forget the strange phenomena of which we have so often heard of late," answered the Doctor, gravely. "At the meetings called 'spirit circles,' invisible hands have been thrust into the hands of those persons round the table – warm, fleshly hands that seemed to pulsate with mortal life."

"What? Do you think, then, that this thing is – "

"I don't know what it is," was the solemn reply.

We watched together, smoking many pipes, all night long, by the bedside of the unearthly being that tossed and panted until it was apparently wearied out. Then we learned by the low, regular breathing that it slept.

The next morning the house was all astir. The boarders congregated on the landing outside my room, and Hammond and myself were lions. We had to answer many questions as to the state of our strange prisoner, for, as yet, not one person except ourselves could be induced to set foot in the apartment.

The creature was awake. This was evidenced by the convulsive manner in which the bedclothes were moved in its efforts to escape.

Hammond and myself had racked our brains during the long night to discover some means by which we might realize the shape and general appearance of the enigma. As well as we could make out by passing our hands over the

16

creature's form, its outlines and lineaments were human. There was a mouth; a round, smooth head without hair; a nose which, however, was little elevated above the cheeks; and its hands and feet felt like those of a boy. At first we thought of placing the being on a smooth surface and tracing its outline with chalk, as shoemakers trace the outline of the foot. This plan was given up as being of no value. Such an outline would give not the slightest idea of its conformation.

A happy thought struck me. We would take a cast of it in plaster of Paris. This would give us the solid figure, and satisfy all our wishes. But how to do it? The movements of the creature would disturb the setting of the plastic covering, and distort the mold. Another thought: Why not give it chloroform? It had respiratory organs – that was evident by its breathing. Once reduced to a state of insensibility, we could do with it what we would. Dr. X— was sent for, and after the worthy physician had recovered from the first shock of amazement, he proceeded to administer the chloroform. In three minutes afterward, we were enabled to remove the fetters from the creature's body, and a well-known modeler of this city was busily engaged in covering the invisible form with the moist clay. In five minutes more we had a mold, and before evening a rough facsimile of the mystery. It was shaped like a man – distorted and horrible, but still a man. It was small, not over four feet in height, and its limbs revealed a muscular development that was unparalleled. Its face surpassed in hideousness anything I had ever seen. Gustave Doré, or Callot, or Tony Johannot, never conceived anything

17

so horrible. There is a face in one of the latter's illustrations to *Un Voyage où il vous plaira*, which somewhat approaches the countenance of this creature, but does not equal it. It was the physiognomy of what I should have fancied a ghoul to be. It looked as if it was capable of feeding on human flesh.

Having satisfied our curiosity, and bound everyone in the house to secrecy, it became a question what was to be done with our enigma. It was impossible that we should keep such a horror in our house. It was equally impossible that such an awful being should be let loose upon the world. I confess that I would have gladly voted for the creature's destruction. But who would shoulder the responsibility? Day after day this question was deliberated gravely.

The boarders all left the house. Mrs. Moffat was in despair, and threatened Hammond and myself with all sorts of legal penalties if we did not remove the horror. Our answer was, "We will go if you like, but we decline taking this creature with us. It appeared in your house. On you the responsibility rests." To this there was, of course, no answer.

The most singular part of the transaction was that we were entirely ignorant of what the creature habitually fed on. Everything in the way of nutriment that we could think of was placed before it, but was never touched. It was awful to stand by, day after day, and see the clothes toss, and hear the hard breathing, and know that it was starving.

Ten, twelve days, a fortnight passed, and it still lived. The pulsations of the heart, however, were daily growing fainter, and had now nearly ceased altogether. It was evident that the creature was dying for want of sustenance. I could not sleep at night. Horrible as the creature was, it was pitiful to think of the pangs it was suffering.

At last it died. Hammond and I found it cold and stiff one morning in the bed. The heart had ceased to beat, the lungs to inspire. We hastened to bury it in the garden. It was a strange funeral, the dropping of that viewless corpse into the damp hole. The cast of its form I gave to Dr. X—, who keeps it in his museum on Tenth Street.

As I am on the eve of a long journey from which I may not return, I have drawn up this narrative of an event – the most singular that has ever come to my knowledge.

DRACULA

Bram Stoker
Extract

I was awakened by the Count, who looked at me as grimly as a man could look as he said, "Tomorrow, my friend, we must part. You return to your beautiful England, I to some work which may have such an end that we may never meet. Your letter home has been dispatched. Tomorrow I shall not be here, but all shall be ready for your journey. In the morning come the Szgany, who have some labors of their own here, and also come some Slovaks. When they have gone, my carriage shall come for you, and shall bear you to the Borgo Pass to meet the diligence from Bukovina to Bistritz. But I am in hopes that I shall see more of you at Castle Dracula."

I suspected him, and determined to test his sincerity. Sincerity! It seems like a profanation of the word to write it in connection with such a monster, so I asked him point-blank, "Why may I not go tonight?"

"Because, dear sir, my coachman and horses are away on a mission."

"But I would walk with pleasure. I want to get away at once."

He smiled, such a soft, smooth, diabolical smile that I knew there was some trick behind it. He said, "And your baggage?"

"I do not care about it. I can send for it some other time."

The Count stood up, and said, with a sweet courtesy which made me rub my eyes, it seemed so real, "You English have a saying which is close to my heart, for its spirit is that which rules our boyars, 'Welcome the coming, speed the parting guest.' Come with me, my dear young friend. Not an hour shall you wait in my house against your will, though sad am I at your going, and that you so suddenly desire it. Come!" With a stately gravity, he, with the lamp, preceded me down the stairs and along the hall. Suddenly he stopped. "Hark!"

Close at hand came the howling of many wolves. It was almost as if the sound sprang up at the rising of his hand, just as the music of a great orchestra seems to leap under the baton of the conductor. After a pause of a moment, he proceeded, in his stately way, to the door, drew back the ponderous bolts, unhooked the heavy chains, and began to draw it open.

To my astonishment, I saw that it was unlocked. Suspiciously, I looked all round, but could see no key of any kind.

As the door began to open, the howling of the wolves outside grew louder and angrier. Their red jaws, with champing teeth, and their blunt-clawed feet as they leaped, came in through the opening door. I knew then that to struggle at the moment against the Count was useless. With such allies as these at his command, I could do nothing.

But still the door continued slowly to open, and only the Count's body stood in the gap. Suddenly it struck me that this might be the moment and means of my doom. I was to be given to the wolves, and at my own instigation. There was a diabolical wickedness in the idea great enough for the Count, and at the last chance I cried out, "Shut the door! I shall wait till morning." And I covered my face with my hands to hide my tears of disappointment.

With one sweep of his powerful arm, the Count threw the door shut, and the great bolts clanged and echoed through the hall.

In silence we returned to the library, and after a minute or two I went to my own room. The last I saw of Count Dracula was his kissing his hand to me, with a red light of triumph in his eyes and a smile that Judas in hell might be proud of.

When I was in my room and about to lie down, I thought I heard a whispering at my door. I went to it softly and listened. Unless my ears deceived me, I heard the voice of the Count.

"Back to your own place! Your time is not yet come. Wait! Have patience! Tonight is mine. Tomorrow night is yours!"

There was a low, sweet ripple of laughter, and in a rage I threw open the door and saw beyond the three terrible women licking their lips. As I appeared, they all joined in a horrible laugh, and ran away.

I came back to my room and threw myself on my knees. It is then so near the end? Tomorrow! Lord, help me!

I slept till just before the dawn, and when I woke threw myself on my knees, for I determined that if Death came he should find me ready.

At last I felt that subtle change in the air, and knew that the morning had come. Then came the welcome cock crow, and I felt that I was safe. With a glad heart, I opened the door and ran down the hall. I had seen that the door was unlocked, and now escape was before me. With hands that trembled with eagerness, I unhooked the chains and threw back the massive bolts.

But the door would not move. Despair seized me. I pulled and pulled at the door, and shook it till, massive as it was, it rattled in its casement. I could see the bolt shot. It had been locked after I left the Count.

Then a wild desire took me to obtain the key at any risk, and I determined then and there to scale the wall again, and gain the Count's room. He might kill me, but death now seemed the happier choice of evils. Without a pause I rushed up to the east window and scrambled down the wall as before, into the Count's room. It was empty, but that was as I expected. I could not see a key anywhere, but the heap of gold remained. I went through the door in the corner and down the winding stair and along the dark passage to the old chapel. I knew now well enough where to find the monster I sought.

The great box was in the same place, close against the wall, but the lid was laid on it, not fastened down, but with the nails ready in their places to be hammered home.

I knew I must search the body for the key, so I raised the lid, and laid it back against the wall. And then I saw something which filled my very soul with horror. There lay the Count, but looking as if his youth had been half restored – for the white hair and mustache were changed to dark iron gray. The cheeks were fuller, and the white skin seemed ruby red underneath. The mouth was redder than ever, for on the lips were gouts of fresh blood, which trickled from the corners of the mouth and ran down over the chin and neck. Even the deep, burning eyes seemed set amongst swollen flesh, for the lids and pouches underneath were bloated. It seemed as if the whole awful creature were simply gorged with blood. He lay like a filthy leech, exhausted with his repletion.

I shuddered as I bent over to touch him and every sense in me revolted at the contact – but I had to search, or I was lost. The coming night might see my own body a banquet in a similar way to those horrid three. I felt all over the body, but no sign could I find of the key. Then I stopped and looked at the Count. There was a mocking smile on the bloated face which seemed to drive me mad. This was the being I was helping to transfer to London, where, perhaps, for centuries to come he might, amongst its teeming millions, satiate his lust for blood, and create a new and ever-widening circle of semi-demons to batten on the helpless.

The very thought drove me mad. A terrible desire came upon me to rid the world of such a monster. There was no lethal weapon at hand, but I seized a shovel that the workmen had been using to fill the cases, and lifting it high, struck, with the edge downward, at the hateful face. But as I did so the head turned, and the eyes fell upon me, with all their blaze of basilisk horror. The sight seemed to paralyze me, and the shovel turned in my hand and glanced from the face, merely making a deep gash above the forehead. The shovel fell from my hand across the box, and as I pulled it away the flange of the blade caught the edge of the lid, which fell over again, and hid the horrid thing from my sight. The last glimpse I had was of the bloated face, bloodstained and fixed with a grin of malice which would have held its own in the nethermost hell.

I thought and thought what should be my next move, but my brain seemed on fire, and I waited with a despairing feeling growing over me. As I waited, I heard in the distance a gipsy song sung by merry voices coming closer, and through their song, the rolling of heavy wheels and the cracking of whips. The Szgany and the Slovaks, of whom the Count had spoken, were coming. With a last look around and at the box that contained the vile body, I ran from the place and gained the Count's room, determined to rush out at the moment the door should be opened. With strained ears, I listened and heard downstairs the grinding of the key in the great lock and the falling back of the heavy door. There must have been some other means of entry, or someone had a key for one of the locked doors.

Then there came the sound of many feet tramping and dying away in some passage which sent up a clanging echo. I turned to run down again toward the vault, where I might find the new entrance, but at the moment there seemed to come a violent puff of wind, and the door to the winding stair blew to with a shock that set the dust from the lintels

flying. When I ran to push it open, I found that it was hopelessly fast. I was again a prisoner, and the net of doom was closing round me.

As I write, there is in the passage below a sound of many tramping feet and the crash of weights being set down heavily, doubtless the boxes, with their freight of earth. There is a sound of hammering. It is the box being nailed down. Now I can hear the heavy feet tramping again along the hall, with many other idle feet coming behind them.

The door is shut; the chains rattle. There is a grinding of the key in the lock. I can hear the key withdrawn, then another door opens and shuts. I hear the creaking of lock and bolt.

Hark! In the courtyard and down the rocky way the roll of heavy wheels, the crack of whips, and the chorus of the Szgany as they pass into the distance.

I am alone in the castle with those horrible women. Faugh! They are devils of the pit!

I shall not remain alone with them. I shall try to scale the castle wall farther than I have yet attempted. I may find a way from this dreadful place.

And then away for home! Away to the quickest and nearest train! Away from the cursed spot, from this cursed land, where the devil and his children still walk with earthly feet!

At least God's mercy is better than that of those monsters, and the precipice is steep and high. At its foot a man may sleep – as a man.

MAN-SIZE IN MARBLE

E. Nesbit

Although every word of this story is as true as despair, I do not expect people to believe it. Nowadays a "rational explanation" is required before belief is possible. Let me then, at once, offer the "rational explanation" which finds most favor among those who have heard the tale of my life's tragedy. It is held that we were "under a delusion," Laura and I, on that 31st of October; and that this supposition places the whole matter on a satisfactory and believable basis. The reader can judge, when he, too, has heard my story, how far this is an "explanation," and in what sense it is "rational." There were three who took part in this; Laura and I and another man. The other man still lives, and can speak to the truth of the least credible part of my story.

I never knew in my life what it was to have as much money as I required to supply the most ordinary needs of life: good colors, canvases, brushes, books, and cab fares and when we were married, we knew quite well that we should only be able to live at all by "strict punctuality and attention to business." I used to paint in those days, and Laura used to write, and we felt sure we could keep the pot at least simmering. Living in town was out of the question, so we went to look for a cottage in the country, which should be at once sanitary and picturesque. So rarely do these two qualities meet in one cottage that our search was for some time quite fruitless. We tried advertisements, but most of the desirable rural residences which we did look at proved to be lacking in both essentials; and when a cottage chanced to have drains, it always had stucco as well and was shaped like a tea caddy. And if we found a vine or rose-covered porch, corruption invariably lurked within. Our minds got so befogged by the eloquence of estate agents, and the rival disadvantages of the fever traps and outrages to beauty which we had seen and scorned, that I very much doubt whether either of us on our wedding morning, knew the difference between a house and a haystack. But when we got away from friends and estate agents, on our honeymoon, our wits grew clear again, and we knew a pretty cottage when at last we saw one.

It was at Brenzett – a little village set on a hill over against the southern marshes. We had gone there, from the seaside village where we were staying, to see the church, and two fields from the church we found this cottage. It stood quite by itself, about two miles from the village. It was a low building with rooms sticking out in unexpected places. There was a bit of stonework – moss-grown – just two old rooms, all that was left of a big house that had once stood there; and round this stone work the house had grown up. It was charming, and after a brief examination we took it. It was absurdly cheap.

The rest of our honeymoon we spent in grubbing about in second-hand shops in the county town, picking up bits of old oak and Chippendale chairs for our furnishing. We wound up with a run up to town and a visit to Liberty's, and soon the low oak-beamed, lattice-windowed rooms began to be home. There was a jolly, old-fashioned garden at the back with grass paths and no end of hollyhocks, sunflowers, and big lilies. From the window you could see the marsh pastures and beyond them the beautiful blue, thin line of the sea.

We were as happy as the summer was glorious, and settled down into work sooner than we ourselves expected. I was never tired of sketching the view and the wonderful cloud effects from the open lattice, and Laura would sit at the table and write verses about them, in which I mostly played the part of foreground.

We got a tall, old peasant woman to housekeep for us. Her face and figure were good, though her cooking was of the homeliest; but she understood all about gardening, and told us all the old names of the coppices and cornfields, the stories of the smugglers and highwaymen, and, better still, of the "things that walked," and of the "sights" which met one in lonely glens of a starlit night. She was a great comfort to us because Laura hated housekeeping as much as I loved folklore, and we soon came to leave all the domestic business to Mrs. Dorman, and to use her legends in little magazine stories which brought in the jingling guinea.

We had three months of married happiness and did not have a single quarrel. One October evening I had been down to smoke a pipe with the doctor – our only neighbor – a pleasant young Irishman. Laura had stayed at home to finish a comic sketch of a village episode for the *Monthly Marplot*. I left her laughing over her own jokes, and came in to find her a crumpled heap of pale muslin weeping on the window seat.

"Good heavens, my darling, what's the matter?" I cried, taking her in my arms. She leaned her little dark head against my shoulder and went on crying. I had never seen her cry before – we had always been so happy, you see – and I felt sure some frightful misfortune had happened.

"What *is* the matter? Do speak."

"It's Mrs. Dorman," she sobbed.

"What has she done?" I inquired, immensely relieved that it was not a serious matter.

"She says she must go before the end of the month, that her niece is ill – she's gone down to see her now – tonight. But I don't believe that's the real, true reason, because her niece is always ill. I believe someone in the village may have been been setting her against us. Her manner was so very peculiar – she was not at all like her usual self."

"Never mind darling," I said. "Whatever you do, don't cry, or I shall have to cry too, to keep you in countenance, and then you'll never respect your man again!"

She dried her eyes obediently on my handkerchief, and even tried to smile, though it was a faint version of her usual pretty one. "But you see," she went on, "it is really serious, because these village people are so sheepy, and if one won't do a thing you may be quite sure none of the others will. And I shall have to cook the dinners and wash up the hateful greasy plates; and you'll have to carry cans of water about, and clean the boots and knives, and we shall never have any time for work, or to earn any money, or anything. We shall have to work hard all day, and only be able to have a slight respite when we are waiting for the kettle to boil!"

I represented to her that even if we had to perform these duties, the day would still present some margin for other toils and recreations; but she would not see the matter in any but the grayest light. She was very unreasonable, but I could not have loved her more if she had been as reasonable as Whately.

"I'll speak to Mrs. Dorman when she comes back, and see if I can't come to terms with her," I said. "Perhaps she only wants a raise in her pay. I am sure it will be all right. Let's walk up to the church together."

The church was a large and lonely one, and we loved to go there, especially upon bright nights. The path skirted a wood, cut through it once, and ran along the crest of the hill through two meadows, and round the churchyard wall, over which the old yews loomed in black masses of shadow. This path, which was partly paved, was called "the bier balk," for it had long been the way by which the corpses had been carried to burial. The churchyard was richly treed, and was shaded by great elms which stood just outside and stretched their majestic arms in benediction over the happy dead. A large, low porch let one into the building by a Norman doorway and a heavy oak door studded with iron.

Inside the arches rose into darkness, and between them, the reticulated windows, which stood out white in the moonlight. In the chancel the windows were of rich glass, which showed in faint light their noble coloring, and made the black oak of the choir pews hardly more solid than the shadows. But on each side of the altar lay a gray marble figure of a knight in full plate armor lying upon a low slab, with hands held up in everlasting prayer. And these figures, oddly enough, were always to be seen if there was even the slightest glimmer of light in the church.

Their names were lost, but the peasants told of them that they had been fierce and wicked men, marauders by land and sea, who had been the scourge of their time, and had been guilty of deeds so foul that the house they had lived in – the big house, by the way, that had stood on the site of our cottage – had been stricken by lightning and the vengeance of heaven. But for all that, the gold of their heirs had bought them a place in the church. Looking at the bad, hard faces reproduced in the marble, this story was easily believed.

The church looked at its best and weirdest on that night, for the shadows of the yew trees fell through the windows upon the floor of the nave and touched the pillars with tattered shade. We sat down together without speaking, and watched the solemn beauty of the old church, with some of that awe which inspired its early builders. We walked to the chancel and looked at the sleeping warriors. Then we rested some time on the stone seat in the porch, looking out over the stretch of quiet moonlit meadows, feeling in every fiber of our being the peace of the night and of our happy love; and came away at last with a sense that even scrubbing and blackleading were but small troubles at their worst.

Mrs. Dorman had come back from the village, and I at once invited her to a *tête-à-tête*. "Now, Mrs. Dorman," I said, when I had got her into my painting room, "what's all this about your not staying with us?"

"I should be glad to get away, sir, before the end of the month," she answered, with her usual placid dignity.

"Have you any fault to find, Mrs. Dorman?"

"None at all, sir. You and your lady have always been most kind, I'm sure —"

"Well, what is it? Are your wages not high enough?"

"No, sir, I gets quite enough."

"Then why not stay?"

"I'd rather not," she said with some hesitation, "my niece is very ill."

"But your niece has been ill ever since we came."

No answer. There was a long and awkward silence. Eventually I broke it.

"Can't you stay for another month?" I asked.

"No, sir. I'm bound to go by Thursday."

And this was Monday!

"Well, I must say, I think you might have let us know before. There's no time now to get anyone else, and your mistress is not fit to do heavy housework. Can't you stay till next week?"

"I might be able to come back next week."

I was now convinced that all she wanted was a brief holiday, which we should have been willing enough to let her have, as soon as we could get a substitute.

"But why must you go this week?" I persisted. "Come, out with it."

Mrs. Dorman drew the little shawl, which she always wore, tightly across her bosom, as though she were cold. Then she said, with a sort of effort: "They say, sir, as this was a big house in Catholic times, and there was a many deeds done here."

The nature of the "deeds" might be vaguely inferred from the inflection of Mrs. Dorman's voice, which was enough to make one's blood run cold. I was glad that Laura was not in the room. She was always nervous, as highly-strung natures are, and I felt that these tales about our house, told by this old peasant woman with her impressive manner and contagious credulity, might have made our home less dear to my wife.

"Tell me all about it, Mrs. Dorman," I said. "You needn't mind about telling me. I'm not like the young people who make fun of such things."

Which was partly true.

"Well, sir," she sank her voice, "you may have seen in the church, beside the altar, two shapes."

"You mean the effigies of the knights in armor," I said cheerfully.

"I mean them two bodies, drawed out man-size in marble," she returned, and I had to admit that her description was a thousand times more graphic than mine, to say nothing of a certain weird force and uncanniness about the phrase "drawed out man-size in marble."

"They do say, as on All Saints' Eve them two bodies sits up on their slabs and gets off of them, and then walks down the aisle, in their marble, and as the church clock strikes eleven they walks out of the church door and along the bier balk, and if it's wet there'll be footprints left in the morning."

"And where do they go?" I asked.

"They comes back here to their home, sir, and if anyone meets them —"

36

"Well, what then?" I asked.

But she only repeated that her niece was ill and she must go. I scorned to discuss the niece, and tried to get from Mrs. Dorman more details of the legend. I could get nothing but warnings.

"Whatever you do, sir, lock the door early on All Saints' Eve, and make the cross sign over the doorstep and on the windows."

"But is there evidence that anyone has ever seen these dreadful things?" I persisted.

"That's not for me to say. I know what I know, sir."

"Well, who was here last year?"

"No one, sir. The lady as owned the house only stayed here in summer, and she always went to London a full month afore the night. And I'm sorry to inconvenience you and your lady, but my niece is ill and I must go on Thursday."

I could have shaken her for her absurd reiteration of that obvious fiction, after she had told me her real reasons. She was determined to go, nor could our united entreaties move her in the least. I did not tell Laura the legend of the shapes that walked in their marble, partly because a legend concerning our house might perhaps trouble my wife, and partly, I think, for some more occult reason. This was not quite the same to me as any other story, and I did not want to talk about it till the day was over. I had very soon ceased to think of the legend, however.

I was painting a portrait of Laura against the lattice window, and I could not think of much else. I had got a splendid background of yellow and gray sunset, and was working away with enthusiasm at her lace.

On Thursday Mrs. Dorman went. She relented, at parting, so far as to say, "Don't you put yourself about too much, ma'am, and if there's any little thing I can do next week, I'm sure I shan't mind," from which I inferred that she wished to come back to us after Halloween. Up to the last, she adhered to the fiction of the niece with touching fidelity.

Thursday passed off pretty well. Laura showed marked ability in the matter of steak and potatoes, and I confess that my knives and the plates, which I insisted upon washing, were better done than I had dared to expect.

Friday came. It is about what happened on that Friday that this is written. I wonder if I should have believed it, if anyone had told it to me. I will write the story of it as quickly and plainly as I can. Everything that happened on that day is burned into my brain. I shall not forget anything, nor leave anything out.

I got up early, I remember, and lit the kitchen fire, and had just achieved a smoky success, when my little wife came running down, as sunny and sweet as the clear October morning itself. We prepared breakfast together, and found it very good fun. The housework was soon done, and when brushes and brooms and pails were quiet again, the house was still indeed. It is wonderful what a difference one makes in a house. We really missed Mrs. Dorman, quite apart from considerations concerning pots and pans. We spent the day in dusting our books and putting them straight, and dined gaily on cold steak and coffee.

Laura was, if possible, brighter and gayer and sweeter than usual, and I began to think that a little domestic toil was really good for her. We had never been so merry since we were married, and the walk we had that afternoon was, I think, the happiest time of all my life. When we had watched the deep scarlet clouds slowly pale into leaden gray against a pale green sky, and saw the white mists curl up along the hedgerows in the distant marsh, we came back to the house, silently, hand in hand.

"You are sad, my darling," I said, half-jestingly, as we sat down together in our little parlor. I expected a disclaimer, for my own silence had been the silence of complete happiness.

To my surprise she said, "Yes. I think I am sad, or rather I am uneasy. I don't think I'm very well. I have shivered three or four times since we came in, and it is not cold, is it?"

"No," I said, and hoped it was not a chill caught from the treacherous mists that roll up from the marshes in the dying light. No she said, she did not think so. Then, after a silence, she spoke suddenly.

"Do you ever have presentiments of evil?"

"No," I said, smiling, "and I shouldn't believe in them even if I had."

"I do," she went on; "the night my father died I knew it, though he was right away in the north of Scotland."

I did not answer in words.

She sat looking at the fire for some time in silence, gently stroking my hand. At last she sprang up, came behind me, and, drawing my head back, kissed me. "There, it's over now," she said. "What a baby I am! Come, light the candles, and we'll have some of these new Rubinstein duets."

And we spent a happy hour or two at the piano.

At about half past ten, I began to long for the goodnight pipe, but Laura looked so white that I felt it would be brutal of me to fill our sitting-room with the fumes of strong cavendish. "I'll take my pipe outside," I said.

"Let me come, too."

"No, sweetheart, not tonight; you're much too tired. I shan't be long. Get to bed, or I shall have an invalid to nurse tomorrow as well as the boots to clean."

I kissed her and was turning to go when she flung her arms round my neck and held me as if she would never let me go again. I stroked her hair.

"Come darling, you're over-tired. The housework has been too much for you."

She loosened her clasp a little and drew a deep breath. "No. We've been very happy today, Jack, haven't we? Don't stay out too long."

"I won't, my dearie."

I strolled out of the front door, leaving it unlatched. What a night it was! The jagged masses of heavy dark cloud were rolling at intervals from horizon to horizon, and thin white wreaths covered the stars. Through all the rush of the cloud river, the moon swam, breasting the waves and disappearing again in the darkness. When now and again her light reached the woodlands, they seemed to be slowly and noiselessly waving in time to the swing of the clouds above them. There was a strange gray light over all the earth; the fields had that shadowy bloom over them, which only comes from the marriage of dew and moonshine, or frost and starlight.

I walked up and down, drinking in the beauty of the quiet earth and the changing sky. The night was absolutely silent. Nothing seemed to be abroad. There was no scurrying of rabbits, or twitter of the half-asleep birds. And though the clouds went sailing across the sky, the wind that drove them never came low enough to rustle the dead leaves in the woodland paths. Across the meadows, I could see the church tower standing out black and gray against the sky. I walked there thinking over our three months of happiness – and of my wife, her dear eyes, her loving ways. Oh, my little girl! My own little girl; what a vision came then of a long, glad life for you and me together!

I heard a bell-beat from the church. Eleven already! I turned to go in, but the night held me. I could not go back into our little warm rooms yet. I would go up to the church. I felt vaguely that it would be good to carry my love and thankfulness to the sanctuary whither so many loads of sorrow and gladness had been borne by the men and women of the dead years.

I looked in at the low window as I went by. Laura was half lying on her chair in front of the fire. I could not see her face; only her little head showed dark against the pale blue wall. She was quite still. Asleep, no doubt. My heart reached out to her, as I went on. There must be a God, I thought, and a God who was good. How otherwise could anything so sweet and dear as she have ever been imagined?

I walked slowly along the edge of the wood. A sound broke the stillness of the night; it was a rustling in the wood. I stopped and listened. The sound stopped too. I went on, and now distinctly heard another step than mine answer mine like an echo. It was a poacher or a wood-stealer, most likely, for these were not unknown in our Arcadian neighborhood. But whoever it was, he was a fool not to step more lightly. I turned into the wood, and now the footstep seemed to come from the path I had just left. It must be an echo, I thought. The wood looked perfect in the moonlight. The large, dying ferns and the brushwood showed where, through thinning foliage, the pale light came down. The tree trunks stood up like Gothic columns all around me. They reminded me of the church, and I turned into the bier balk and passed through the corpse gate between the graves to the low porch. I paused for a moment on the stone seat where Laura and I had watched the fading landscape. Then I noticed that the door of the church was open, and I blamed myself for having left it unlatched the other night. We were the only people who ever cared to come to the church except on Sundays, and I was vexed to think that through our carelessness the damp autumn airs had had a chance of getting in and injuring the old fabric. I went in. It will seem strange, perhaps, that I should have gone halfway up the aisle before I remembered with a sudden chill, followed by as sudden a rush of self-contempt that this was the very day and hour when, according to tradition, the shapes drawed out man-size in marble began to walk.

Having thus remembered the legend, and remembered it with a shiver, of which I was ashamed, I could not do otherwise than walk up toward the altar – just to look at the figures – as I said to myself; really what I wanted was to assure myself, first, that I did not believe the legend, and, secondly, that it was not true. I was rather glad that I had come. I thought now I could tell Mrs. Dorman how vain her fancies were, and how peacefully the marble figures slept on through the ghastly hour. With my hands in my pockets, I passed up the aisle. In the gray dim light the eastern end of the church looked larger than usual, and the arches above the two tombs looked larger, too. The moon came out and showed me the reason. I stopped short, my heart gave a leap that nearly choked me, and then sank sickeningly.

The "bodies drawed out man-size" *were gone*, and their marble slabs lay wide and bare in the vague moonlight that slanted through the east window.

Were they really gone? Or was I mad? Clenching my nerves, I stooped and passed my hand over the smooth slabs, and felt their flat unbroken surface. Had someone taken the things away? Was it some vile practical joke? I would make sure, anyway. In an instant I had made a torch of a newspaper, which happened to be in my pocket, and, lighting it, held it high above my head. Its yellow glare illumined the dark arches and those slabs. The figures were gone. And I was alone in the church; or was I alone?

And then a horror seized me, a horror indefinable and indescribable – an overwhelming certainty of supreme and accomplished calamity. I flung down the torch and tore along the aisle and out through the porch, biting my lips as I ran to keep myself from shrieking aloud. Oh, was I mad – or what was this that possessed me? I leapt the churchyard wall and took the straight cut across the fields, led by the light from our windows. Just as I got over the first stile, a dark figure seemed to spring out of the ground. Mad still with that certainty of misfortune, I made for the thing that stood in my path, shouting, "Get out of the way, can't you!"

But my push met with a more vigorous resistance than I had expected. My arms were caught just above the elbow and held as in a vice, and the raw-boned Irish doctor actually shook me.

"Would ye?" he cried, in his own unmistakable accents – "would ye, then?"

"Let me go, you fool," I gasped. "The marble figures have gone from the church; I tell you they've gone."

He broke into a ringing laugh. "I'll have to give ye a draft tomorrow, I see. Ye've listening to old wives' tales."

"I tell you, I've seen the bare slabs."

"Well, come back with me. I'm going up to old Palmer's; his daughter's ill. We'll look in at the church and let me see the bare slabs."

"You go, if you like," I said, a little less frantic for his laughter. "I'm going home to my wife."

"Rubbish, man," said he. "D'ye think I'll permit of that? Are ye to go saying all yer life that ye've seen solid marble endowed with vitality, and me to go all me life saying ye were a coward? No, sir ye shan't do ut."

The night air, a human voice, and I think also the physical contact with this six feet of solid common sense, brought me back a little to my ordinary self, and the word 'coward' was a mental shower-bath.

"Come on, then," I said sullenly, "perhaps you're right."

He still held my arm tightly. We got over the stile and back to the church. All was still as death. The place smelt very

45

damp and earthy. We walked up the aisle. I am not ashamed to confess that I shut my eyes: I knew the figures would not be there. I heard Kelly strike a match.

"Here they are, ye see, right enough; ye've been dreaming or drinking, asking yer pardon for the imputation."

I opened my eyes. By Kelly's expiring vesta, I saw two shapes lying 'in their marble' on their slabs. I drew a deep breath, and caught his hand.

"I'm awfully indebted to you," I said. "It must have been some trick of light, or I have been working rather hard, perhaps that's it. Do you know, I was quite convinced they were gone."

"I'm aware of that," he answered, rather grimly, "ye'll have to be careful of that brain of yours, my friend, I assure ye."

He was leaning over and looking at the right-hand figure, whose stony face was the most villainous and deadly in expression.

"By Jove," he said, "something has been afoot here – this hand is broken."

And so it was. I was certain that it had been perfect the last time Laura and I had been there.

"Perhaps someone has tried to remove them," said the young doctor.

"That won't account for my impression," I objected.

"Too much painting and not enough rest will account for that, well enough."

"Come along," I said, "or my wife will be getting anxious. You'll come in and have a drop of whisky and drink confusion to ghosts and better sense to me."

46

"I ought to go up to Palmer's, but it's so late now I'd best leave it till the morning," he replied. "I was kept late at the Union, and I've had to see a lot of people since. All right, I'll come back with ye."

I think he fancied I needed him more than did Palmer's girl, so, discussing how such an illusion could have been possible, and deducing from this experience large generalities concerning ghostly apparitions, we walked up to our cottage. We saw, as we walked up the garden path, that bright light streamed out of the front door, and presently saw that the parlor door was open too. Had she gone out?

"Come in," I said, and Dr. Kelly followed me into the parlor. It was ablaze with candles, not only the wax ones, but at least a dozen guttering, tallow dips, stuck in vases and ornaments in unlikely places. Light was Laura's remedy for nervousness. Poor child! Why had I left her? Brute that I was.

We glanced round the room, and at first we did not see her. The window was open, and the draft set all the candles flaring one way. Her chair was empty and her handkerchief and book lay on the floor. I turned to the window. There, in the recess of the window, I saw her. Oh, my child, my love, had she gone to that window to watch for me? And what had come into the room behind her? To what had she turned with that look of frantic fear and horror? Oh, my little one, had she thought that it was I whose step she heard, and turned to meet what?

She had fallen back across a table in the window, and her body lay half on it and half on the window seat, and her head hung down over the table, the brown hair loosened and fallen to the carpet. Her lips were drawn back, and her eyes wide open. They saw nothing now. What had they seen last?

The doctor moved toward her, but I pushed him aside and sprang to her; caught her in my arms and cried: "It's all right, Laura! I've got you safe darling." She fell into my arms in a heap. I clasped her and kissed her, and called her name, but I think I knew all the time that she was dead. Her hands were

tightly clenched. In one of them she held something fast. When I was quite sure that she was dead, and that nothing mattered at all any more, I let him open her hand to see what she held.

It was a gray marble finger.

THE HOUND OF THE BASKERVILLES

Sir Arthur Conan Doyle

Extract

I have said that over the great Grimpen Mire there hung a dense, white fog. It was drifting slowly in our direction and banked itself up like a wall on that side of us, low but thick and well defined. The moon shone on it, and it looked like a great, shimmering ice field. Holmes' face was turned toward it, and he muttered impatiently as he watched its sluggish drift.

"It's moving toward us, Watson."

"Is that serious?"

"Very serious, indeed – the one thing upon earth which could have disarranged my plans. He can't be very long, now. It is already ten o'clock. Our success and even his life may depend upon his coming out before the fog is over the path."

The night was clear and fine. The stars shone cold and bright, while a half-moon bathed the whole scene in a soft, uncertain light. Before us lay the dark bulk of the house, its serrated roof and bristling chimneys hard outlined against the silver-spangled sky. Broad bars of golden light from the lower windows stretched across the orchard and the moor. One of them was suddenly shut off. There only remained the lamp in the dining room where the two men, the murderous host – and the unconscious guest – still chatted over their cigars.

Every minute, that white woolly plain that covered one half of the moor was drifting closer and closer to the house. Already the first thin wisps of it were curling across the golden square of the lighted window. The farther wall of the orchard was already invisible, and the trees were standing out of a swirl of white vapor. As we watched it, the fog wreaths came crawling round both corners of the house and rolled slowly into one dense bank on which the upper floor and the roof floated like a strange ship upon a shadowy sea. Holmes struck his hand passionately upon the rock in front of us and stamped his feet in his impatience.

"If he isn't out in a quarter of an hour, the path will be covered. In half an hour we won't be able to see our hands."

"Shall we move farther back upon higher ground?"

"Yes, I think it would be as well."

So as the fog bank flowed onward, we fell back before it until we were half a mile from the house, our footsteps crunching in the remains of the snow, and still that dense white sea, with the moon silvering its upper edge, swept on.

"We are going too far," said Holmes. "We dare not take the chance of his being overtaken before he can reach us. At all costs we must hold our ground where we are." He dropped

51

on his knees and clapped his ear to the ground. "Thank God, I think that I hear him coming."

A sound of quick steps broke the silence of the moor. Crouching among the stones we stared intently at the silver-tipped bank in front of us. The steps grew louder, and through the fog, as through a curtain, there stepped the man whom we were awaiting. He looked round him in surprise as he emerged into the clear, starlit night. Then he came swiftly along the path, passed close to where we lay, and went on up the long slope behind us. As he walked he glanced continually over either shoulder, like a man who is ill at ease.

"Hist!" cried Holmes, and I heard the sharp click of a cocking pistol. "Look out! It's coming!"

There was a thin, crisp, continuous patter from somewhere in the heart of that crawling bank. The cloud was within fifty yards of where we lay, and we glared at it, all three, uncertain what horror was about to break from the heart of it. I was at Holmes's elbow, and I glanced at his face. It was pale and exultant, his eyes shining brightly in the moonlight. But suddenly they started forward in a rigid, fixed stare, and his lips parted in amazement. At the same instant, Lestrade gave a yell of terror and threw himself face downward upon the ground.

I sprang to my feet, my inert hand grasping my pistol, my mind paralyzed by the dreadful shape that had sprung out upon us from the shadows of the fog. A hound it was, an enormous, coal-black hound, but not such a hound as mortal eyes have ever seen. Fire burst from its open mouth, its eyes glowed with a smoldering glare, its muzzle and hackles and dewlap were outlined in flickering flame. Never could anything more savage, more hellish be conceived than that dark form and savage face which broke upon us out of the wall of fog.

With long bounds, the huge black creature was leaping down the track, following hard upon the footsteps of our friend. So paralyzed were we by the apparition that we allowed him to pass before we had recovered our nerve. Then Holmes and I both fired together, and the creature gave a hideous howl, which showed that one at least had hit him. He did not pause, however, but bounded onward. Far away on the path we saw Sir Henry looking back, his face white in the moonlight, his hands raised in horror, glaring helplessly at the frightful thing.

But that cry of pain from the hound had blown all our fears to the winds. If he was vulnerable he was mortal, and if we could wound him we could kill him. Never have I seen a man run as Holmes ran that night. I am reckoned fleet of foot, but he outpaced me as much as I outpaced the little professional. In front of us as we flew up the track we heard scream after scream from Sir Henry and the deep roar of the hound. I was in time to see the beast spring upon its victim, hurl him to the ground, and worry at his throat. But the next instant Holmes had emptied five barrels of his revolver into the creature's flank. With a last howl of agony and a vicious snap in the air, it rolled upon its back, four feet pawing furiously, and then fell limp upon its side. The giant hound was dead.

Sir Henry lay insensible where he had fallen. We tore away his collar, and Holmes breathed a prayer of gratitude when we saw that there was no sign of a wound and that the rescue had been in time. Already our friend's eyelids shivered. Lestrade thrust his brandy flask between the baronet's teeth, and two frightened eyes were looking up at us.

"My God!" he whispered. "Whatever was it?"

"It's dead, whatever it is," said Holmes. "We've laid the family ghost once and forever."

CARMILLA

J. Sheridan Le Fanu

Extract

The old general's eyes were fixed on the ground, as he leaned with his hand upon the basement of a shattered monument.

Under a narrow, arched doorway, surmounted by one of those demoniacal grotesques in which the cynical and ghastly fancy of old Gothic carving delights, I saw very gladly the beautiful face and figure of Carmilla enter the shadowy chapel.

I was just about to rise and speak, having nodded, smiling, in answer to her peculiarly engaging smile; when with a cry, the old man by my side caught up the woodman's hatchet, and started forward. On seeing him, a brutalized change came over her features. It was an instantaneous and horrible transformation, as she made a crouching step backward. Before I could utter a scream, he struck at her with all his force; but she dived under his blow, and unscathed, caught him in her tiny grasp by the wrist. He struggled for a moment to release his arm, but his hand opened, the axe fell to the ground, and the girl was gone.

He staggered against the wall. His gray hair stood upon his head, and a moisture shone over his face, as if he were at the point of death.

The frightful scene had passed in a moment. The first thing I recollect after is *madame* standing before me, and impatiently repeating again and again the question, "Where is Mademoiselle Carmilla?"

I answered at length, "I don't know – I can't tell – she went there," and I pointed to the door through which *madame* had just entered, "only a minute or two since."

"But I have been standing there, in the passage, ever since Mademoiselle Carmilla entered, and she did not return."

She then began to call Carmilla, through every door and passage and from the windows, but no answer came.

"She called herself Carmilla?" asked the general, still agitated.

"Carmilla, yes," I answered.

"Aye," he said, "that is Millarca. That is the same person who long ago was called many other names – Mircalla, Countess Karnstein. Depart from this accursed ground, my poor child, as quickly as you can. Drive to the clergyman's house, and stay there till we come. Only there will you be safe. Begone! May you never behold Carmilla more; for you will not see her face here again."

As he spoke, one of the strangest-looking men I ever beheld entered the chapel at the door through which Carmilla had made her entrance and her exit. He was tall, narrow-chested, stooping, with high shoulders, and dressed in black. His face was brown and dried in with deep furrows, and he wore an oddly-shaped hat with a broad leaf. His hair, long and grizzled, hung on his shoulders. He wore a pair of gold spectacles, and walked slowly with an odd, shambling gait. With his face sometimes turned up to the sky and sometimes bowed down toward the ground, he seemed to wear a perpetual smile. His long, thin arms were swinging, and his lank hands, in old black gloves ever so much too wide for them, waving and gesticulating in utter abstraction. "The very man!" exclaimed the general, advancing with manifest delight. "My dear baron, how happy I am to see you; I had no hope of meeting you so soon." He signed to my father, who had by this time returned, and leading the fantastic old gentleman, whom he called the baron, to meet him, he introduced him formally, and they at once entered into earnest conversation. The stranger took a roll of paper from his pocket, and spread it on the worn surface of a tomb that stood by. He had a pencil case in his fingers, with which he traced imaginary lines from point to point on the paper, which, from their often glancing from it together at certain points of the building, I concluded to be a plan of the chapel. He accompanied what I may term his lecture, with occasional readings from a dirty little book, whose yellow leaves were closely written over.

They sauntered together down the side aisle, opposite to the spot where I was standing, conversing as they went. Then they began measuring distances by paces, and finally they all stood together, facing a piece of the sidewall, which they began to examine with great minuteness – pulling off the ivy that clung over it, and rapping the plaster with the ends of their sticks, scraping here, and knocking there. At length they ascertained the existence of a broad marble tablet, with letters carved in relief upon it.

With the assistance of the woodman, who soon returned, a monumental inscription, and carved coat-of-arms, were disclosed. They proved to be those of the long-lost monument of Mircalla, Countess Karnstein.

The old general, though not, I fear, given to the praying mood, raised his hands and eyes to heaven, in mute thanksgiving for some moments.

"Tomorrow," I heard him say; "the commissioner will be here, and the inquisition will be held according to law."

Then turning to the old man with the gold spectacles, whom I have described, he shook him warmly by both hands and said: "How can I thank you? How can we all thank you? You will have delivered this region from a plague that has scourged its inhabitants for more than a century. The horrible enemy, thank God, is at last tracked."

My father led the stranger aside, and the general followed. I knew that he had led them out of hearing, that he might relate my case, and I saw them glance often quickly at me, as the discussion proceeded.

My father came to me, kissed me again and again, and leading me from the chapel, said, "It is time to return, but before we go home, we must add to our party the good priest, who lives but a little way from this, and persuade him to accompany us to the *schloss*."

In this quest we were successful, and I was glad, being unspeakably fatigued when we reached home. But my satisfaction was changed to dismay, on discovering that there were no tidings of Carmilla. Of the scene that had occurred in the ruined chapel, no explanation was offered to me, and it was clear that it was a secret which my father, for the present, determined to keep from me.

The sinister absence of Carmilla made the remembrance of the scene more horrible to me. The arrangements for the night were singular. Two servants and *madame* were to sit up in my room that night; and the ecclesiastic with my father kept watch in the adjoining dressing room.

The priest had performed certain solemn rites that night, the purport of which I did not understand any more than I comprehended the reason of this extraordinary precaution taken for my safety during sleep.

I saw all clearly a few days later.

The disappearance of Carmilla was followed by the discontinuance of my nightly sufferings.

You have heard, no doubt, of the appalling superstition that prevails in Upper and Lower Styria, in Moravia, Silesia, in Turkish Servia, in Poland, even in Russia; the superstition, so we must call it, of the vampire.

If human testimony – taken with every care and solemnity, judicially, before commissions innumerable, each consisting of many members all chosen for integrity and intelligence, and constituting reports more voluminous perhaps than exist upon any one other class of cases – is worth anything, it is difficult to deny, or even to doubt the existence of such a phenomenon as the vampire.

For my part, I have heard no theory by which to explain what I myself have witnessed and experienced, other than that supplied by the ancient and well-attested belief of the country.

The next day the formal proceedings took place in the Chapel of Karnstein. The grave of the Countess Mircalla was opened, and the general and my father recognized each his perfidious and beautiful guest, in the face now disclosed to view. The features, though a hundred and fifty years had passed since her funeral, were tinted with the warmth of life. No cadaverous smell exhaled from the coffin. The two medical men, one officially present, the other there on the

part of the promoter of the inquiry, attested the marvelous fact that there was a faint but appreciable respiration, and a corresponding action of the heart. The limbs were perfectly flexible, the flesh elastic, and the leaden coffin floated with blood. Here then, were all the admitted signs and proofs of vampirism. The body therefore, in accordance with the ancient practice, was raised and a sharp stake driven through the heart of the vampire, who uttered a piercing shriek at the moment, in all respects such as might escape from a living person in the last agony. Then the head was struck off, and a torrent of blood flowed from the severed neck. The body and head were next placed on a pile of wood, and reduced to ashes, which were thrown upon the river and borne away; and that territory has never since been plagued by the visits of a vampire.

My father has a copy of the report of the Imperial Commission, with the signatures of all who were present at these proceedings, attached in verification of the statement. It is from this official paper that I have summarized my account of this last shocking scene.

THE MASQUE OF THE RED DEATH

Edgar Allan Poe

The "Red Death" had long devastated the country. No pestilence had ever been so fatal. Blood was its Avatar and its seal – the redness and the horror of blood. There were sharp pains, and sudden dizziness, and then profuse bleeding at the pores, with dissolution. The scarlet stains upon the body and especially upon the face of the victim, were the pest ban which shut him out from the aid and from the sympathy of his fellow men. And the whole seizure, progress, and termination of the disease, were the incidents of half an hour.

But the Prince Prospero was happy and dauntless and sagacious. When his dominions were half depopulated, he summoned to his presence a thousand hale and light-hearted friends from among the knights and dames of his court, and with these retired to the deep seclusion of one of his castellated abbeys. This was an extensive and magnificent structure, the creation of the prince's own eccentric yet august taste. A strong and lofty wall girdled it in. This wall had gates of iron. The courtiers, having entered, brought furnaces and massy hammers and welded the bolts. They resolved to leave means neither of ingress nor egress to the sudden impulses of despair or of frenzy from within. The abbey was amply provisioned. With such precautions the courtiers might bid defiance to contagion. The external world could take care of itself. In the meantime it was folly to grieve, or to think. The prince had provided all the appliances of pleasure. There were buffoons, there were improvisatori, there were ballet dancers, there were musicians, there was beauty, there was wine. All these and security were within. Without was the "Red Death."

It was toward the close of the fifth month of his seclusion, while the pestilence raged furiously, that the Prince Prospero entertained his friends at a masked ball of unusual magnificence.

It was a voluptuous scene, that masquerade. But first let me tell of the rooms in which it was held. There were seven – an imperial suite. The apartments were so irregularly disposed that the vision embraced but little more than one at a time. There was a sharp turn at every twenty or thirty yards, and at each turn a novel effect. To the right and left, in the middle of each wall, a tall and narrow Gothic window looked out upon a closed corridor which pursued the windings of the suite. These windows were of stained glass whose color varied in accordance with the prevailing hue of

the decorations of the chamber into which it opened. That at the eastern extremity was hung, for example, in blue – and vividly blue were its windows. The second chamber was purple in its ornaments and tapestries, and here the panes were purple. The third was green throughout, and so were the casements. The fourth was furnished and lit with orange – the fifth with white – the sixth with violet. The seventh apartment was closely shrouded in black velvet tapestries that hung all over the ceiling and down the walls, falling in heavy folds upon a carpet of the same material and hue. But in this chamber only, the color of the windows failed to correspond with the decorations. The panes here were scarlet – a deep blood color. Now in no one of the seven apartments was there any lamp or candelabrum, amid the profusion of golden ornaments that lay scattered to and fro or depended from the roof. There was no light of any kind emanating from lamp or candle within the suite of chambers. But in the corridors that followed the suite, there stood, opposite to each window, a heavy tripod, bearing a brazier of fire that projected its rays through the tinted glass and so glaringly illumined the room. And thus were produced a multitude of gaudy and fantastic appearances. But in the western or black chamber, the effect of the firelight that streamed upon the dark hangings through the blood-tinted panes was ghastly in the extreme, and produced so wild a look upon the countenances of those who entered, that there were few of the company bold enough to set foot within its precincts at all.

It was in this apartment, also, that there stood against the western wall a gigantic clock of ebony. Its pendulum swung to and fro with a dull, heavy, monotonous clang; and when the minute hand made the circuit of the face, and the hour was to be stricken, there came from the brazen lungs of the clock a sound which was clear and loud and deep and exceedingly musical, but of so peculiar a note and emphasis that, at each lapse of an hour, the musicians of the orchestra were constrained to pause, momentarily, in their performance, to hearken to the sound; and thus the waltzers perforce ceased their evolutions; and there was a brief disconcert of the whole merry company. And, while the chimes of the clock yet rang, it was observed that the giddiest grew pale, and the more aged and sedate passed their hands over their brows as if in confused reverie or meditation. But when the echoes had fully ceased, a light laughter at once pervaded the assembly. The musicians looked at each other and smiled as if at their own nervousness and folly, and made whispering vows, each to the other, that the next chiming of the clock should produce in them no similar emotion. And then, after the lapse of sixty minutes – which embrace three thousand and

six hundred seconds of the Time that flies – there came
yet another chiming of the clock, and then were the same
disconcert and tremulousness and meditation as before.

But, in spite of these things, it was a magnificent revel.
The tastes of the duke were peculiar. He had a fine eye for
colors and effects. His plans were bold and fiery, and his
conceptions glowed with barbaric luster. There are some
who would have thought him mad. His followers felt he was
not. It was necessary to hear, see, and touch him to be sure
that he was not.

He had directed, in great part, the movable
embellishments of the seven chambers upon occasion
of this great *fête*; and it was his own guiding taste which
had given character to the masqueraders. Be sure they were
grotesque. There were much glare and glitter and piquancy
and phantasm. There were arabesque figures with unsuited
limbs and appointments. There were delirious fancies such
as the madman fashions.

There was much of the beautiful, much of the wanton,
much of the bizarre, something of the terrible, and not a little
of that which might have excited disgust. To and fro in the
seven chambers there stalked, in fact, a multitude of dreams.
And these – the dreams – writhed in and about, taking hue
from the rooms, and causing the wild music of the orchestra
to seem as the echo of their steps.

And, anon, there strikes the ebony clock which stands in
the hall of the velvet. And then, for a moment, all is still, and
all is silent save the voice of the clock. The dreams are stiff-

frozen as they stand. But the echoes of the chime die away – they have endured but an instant – and a light, half-subdued laughter floats after them as they depart.

And now again the music swells, and the dreams live and writhe to and fro more merrily than ever, taking hue from the tinted windows through which stream the rays from the tripods. But to the chamber which lies most westwardly of the seven, there are now none of the masquers who venture. For the night is waning away; and there flows a ruddier light through the blood-colored panes; and the blackness of the sable drapery appalls. And to him whose foot falls upon the sable carpet, there comes from the near clock of ebony a muffled peal more solemnly emphatic than any which reaches *their* ears who indulge in the more remote gaieties of the other apartments.

But these other apartments were densely crowded, and in them beat feverishly the heart of life. And the revel went whirlingly on, until at length there commenced the sounding of midnight upon the clock. And then the music ceased, as I have told; and the evolutions of the waltzers were quieted; and there was an uneasy cessation of all things as before. But now there were twelve strokes to be sounded by the bell of the clock; and thus it happened, that more of thought crept, with more of time, into the meditations of the thoughtful among those who reveled. And thus, too, it happened, perhaps, that before the last echoes of the last chime had utterly sunk into silence, there were many individuals in the crowd who had found leisure to become aware of the presence of a masked figure that had arrested the attention of no single individual before. And the rumor of this new presence having spread itself whisperingly around, there arose at length from the whole company a buzz, or murmur, expressive of disapprobation and surprise – then, finally, of terror, of horror, and of disgust.

In an assembly of phantasms such as I have painted, it may well be supposed that no ordinary appearance could have excited such sensation. In truth the masquerade license of the night was nearly unlimited; but the figure in question had gone beyond the bounds of even the prince's indefinite decorum. There are chords in the hearts of the most reckless which cannot be touched without emotion. Even with the utterly lost, to whom life and death are equally jests, there are matters of which no jest can be made. The whole company, indeed, seemed now deeply to feel that in the costume and bearing of the stranger neither wit nor propriety existed. The figure was tall and gaunt, and shrouded from head to foot in the garments of the grave. The mask that concealed the visage was made so nearly to resemble the countenance of a stiffened corpse that the closest scrutiny must have had difficulty in detecting the cheat. And yet all this might have been endured, if not approved, by the mad revelers around. But the mummer had gone so far as to assume the type of the Red Death. His vesture was dabbled in blood – and his brow, with the features of the face, was besprinkled with the scarlet horror.

When the eyes of Prince Prospero fell upon this spectral image (which with a slow and solemn movement, as if more fully to sustain its role, stalked to and fro among the waltzers) he was seen to be convulsed, in the first moment with a strong shudder either of terror or distaste; but, in the next, his brow reddened with rage.

"Who dares?" he demanded hoarsely of the courtiers who stood near him. "Who dares insult us with this blasphemous mockery? Seize him and unmask him, that we may know whom we have to hang at sunrise!"

It was in the eastern or blue chamber in which stood the Prince Prospero as he uttered these words. They rang throughout the seven rooms loudly and clearly – for the prince was a bold and robust man, and the music had become hushed at the waving of his hand.

At first, as he spoke, there was a slight rushing movement of the courtiers in the direction of the intruder, who at the moment was also near at hand, and now, with deliberate and stately step, made closer approach to the speaker. But from a certain nameless awe with which the mad assumptions of the mummer had inspired the whole party, there were found none who put forth hand to seize him; so that, unimpeded, he passed within a yard of the prince's person. And, while the vast assembly, as if with one impulse, shrank from the centers of the rooms to the walls, he made his way uninterruptedly, but with the same solemn and measured step which had distinguished him from the first, through the blue chamber to the purple – through the purple to the green – through the green to the orange – through this again to the white – and even thence to the violet, ere a decided movement had been made to arrest him. It was then, however, that the Prince Prospero, maddening with rage and the shame of his own momentary cowardice, rushed hurriedly through the six chambers – while none followed him on account of a deadly terror that had seized upon all. He bore aloft a drawn dagger, and had approached to within three or four feet of the retreating figure, when the latter turned suddenly and confronted his pursuer. There was a sharp cry – and the dagger dropped gleaming upon the sable carpet, upon which, instantly afterward, fell prostrate in death the Prince Prospero. Then, summoning the wild courage of despair, a throng of the revelers at once threw themselves into the black apartment, and, seizing the mummer – whose tall figure stood erect and motionless within the shadow of the ebony clock – gasped in unutterable horror at finding the burial clothes and corpse-like mask which they handled with so violent a rudeness, untenanted by any tangible form.

And now was acknowledged the presence of the Red Death. He had come like a thief in the night. And one by one dropped the revelers in the blood-bedewed halls of their revel, and died each in the despairing posture of his fall. And the life of the ebony clock went out with that of the last of the merry. And the flames of the tripods expired. And darkness and decay and the Red Death held illimitable dominion over all.

THE PICTURE OF DORIAN GRAY

Oscar Wilde

For some reason or other, the house was crowded that night, and the fat manager who met them at the door was beaming from ear to ear with an oily, tremulous smile. He escorted them to their box with a sort of pompous humility, waving his fat, jewelled hands and talking at the top of his voice. Dorian Gray loathed him more than ever. He felt as if he had come to look for Miranda and had been met by Caliban. Lord Henry, upon the other hand, rather liked him. At least he declared he did, and insisted on shaking him by the hand and assuring him that he was proud to meet a man who had discovered a real genius and gone bankrupt over a poet. Hallward amused himself with watching the faces in the pit. The heat was terribly oppressive, and the huge sunlight flamed like a monstrous dahlia with petals of yellow fire. The youths in the gallery had taken off their coats and waistcoats and hung them over the side. The sound of the popping of corks came from the bar.

"What a place to find one's divinity in!" said Lord Henry.

"Yes!" answered Dorian Gray. "It was here I found her, and she is divine beyond all living things. When she acts, you will forget everything. These common rough people, with their coarse faces and brutal gestures, become quite different when she is on the stage. They sit silently and watch her. They weep and laugh as she wills them to do. She makes them as responsive as a violin. She spiritualizes them, and one feels that they are of the same flesh and blood as one's self."

"The same flesh and blood as one's self! Oh, I hope not!" exclaimed Lord Henry, who was scanning the occupants of the gallery through his opera glass.

"Don't pay any attention to him, Dorian," said the painter. "I understand what you mean, and I believe in this girl. Anyone you love must be marvelous. If this girl can give a soul to those who have lived without one, if she can create the sense of beauty in people whose lives have been sordid and ugly, if she can strip them of their selfishness and lend them tears for sorrows that are not their own, she is worthy of all your adoration. This marriage is quite right. I did not think so at first, but I admit it now. The gods made Sibyl Vane for you. Without her you would have been incomplete."

"Thanks, Basil," answered Dorian Gray, pressing his hand. "I knew that you would understand me. Harry is so cynical, he terrifies me. But here is the orchestra. It is quite dreadful, but it only lasts for about five minutes. Then the curtain rises,

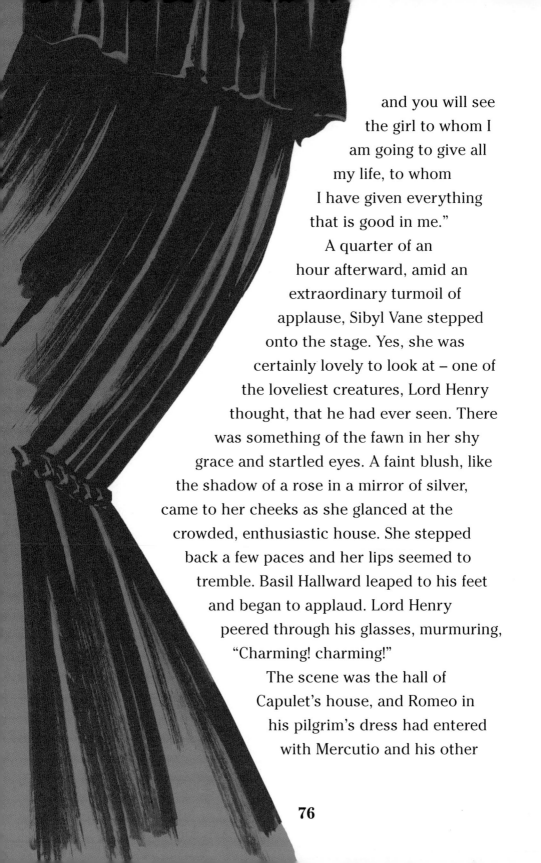

and you will see
the girl to whom I
am going to give all
my life, to whom
I have given everything
that is good in me."
A quarter of an
hour afterward, amid an
extraordinary turmoil of
applause, Sibyl Vane stepped
onto the stage. Yes, she was
certainly lovely to look at – one of
the loveliest creatures, Lord Henry
thought, that he had ever seen. There
was something of the fawn in her shy
grace and startled eyes. A faint blush, like
the shadow of a rose in a mirror of silver,
came to her cheeks as she glanced at the
crowded, enthusiastic house. She stepped
back a few paces and her lips seemed to
tremble. Basil Hallward leaped to his feet
and began to applaud. Lord Henry
peered through his glasses, murmuring,
"Charming! charming!"
The scene was the hall of
Capulet's house, and Romeo in
his pilgrim's dress had entered
with Mercutio and his other

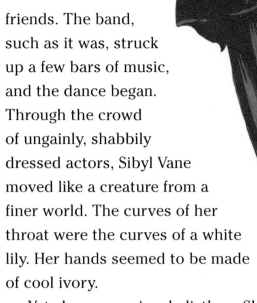

friends. The band,
such as it was, struck
up a few bars of music,
and the dance began.
Through the crowd
of ungainly, shabbily
dressed actors, Sibyl Vane
moved like a creature from a
finer world. The curves of her
throat were the curves of a white
lily. Her hands seemed to be made
of cool ivory.

Yet she was curiously listless. She
showed no sign of joy when her eyes
rested on Romeo. The few words she
had to speak were spoken in a thoroughly
artificial manner. The voice was exquisite,
but from the point of view of tone it was
absolutely false. It was wrong in color. It took
away all the life from the verse.
It made the passion unreal.

Dorian Gray grew pale as he
watched her. He was puzzled and
anxious. Neither of his friends
dared to say anything to him. She
seemed to them to be absolutely
incompetent. They were
horribly disappointed.

Yet they felt that the true test of any Juliet is the balcony scene of the second act. If she failed there, there was nothing in her.

She looked charming as she came out in the moonlight. That could not be denied. But the staginess of her acting was unbearable, and grew worse as she went on. Her gestures became absurdly artificial. She overemphasized everything that she had to say. The beautiful passage:

Thou knowest the mask of night is on my face,
Else would a maiden blush bepaint my cheek
For that which thou hast heard me speak tonight

was declaimed with the painful precision of a schoolgirl who has been taught to recite by some second-rate professor of elocution. When she leaned over the balcony and came to those wonderful lines:

Although I joy in thee,
I have no joy of this contract to-night:
It is too rash, too unadvised, too sudden;
Too like the lightning, which doth cease to be
Ere one can say, "It lightens." Sweet, goodnight!
This bud of love by summer's ripening breath
May prove a beauteous flower when next we meet

she spoke the words as though they conveyed no meaning to her. It was not nervousness. Indeed, so far from being nervous, she was absolutely self-contained. It was simply bad art. She was a complete failure.

Even the common, uneducated audience of the pit and gallery lost their interest in the play. They got restless, and began to talk loudly and to whistle. The manager, who was standing at the back of the dress circle, stamped and swore with rage. The only person unmoved was the girl herself.

When the second act was over, there came a storm of hisses, and Lord Henry got up from his chair and put on his coat. "She is quite beautiful, Dorian," he said, "but she can't act. Let us go."

"I am going to see the play through," answered the lad, in a hard, bitter voice. "I am awfully sorry that I have made you waste an evening, Harry. I apologize to you both."

"My dear Dorian, I should think Miss Vane was ill," interrupted Hallward. "We will come some other night."

"I wish she were ill," he rejoined. "But she seems to me to be simply callous and cold. She has entirely altered. Last night she was a great artist. This evening she is merely a commonplace, mediocre actress."

"Don't talk like that about anyone you love, Dorian. Love is a more wonderful thing than art."

"They are both simply forms of imitation," remarked Lord Henry. "But do let us go. Dorian, you must not stay here any longer. It is not good for one's morals to see bad acting. Besides, I don't suppose you will want your wife to act, so what does it matter if she plays Juliet like a wooden doll? She is very lovely, and if she knows as little about life as she does about acting, she will be a delightful experience. Good heavens, my dear boy, don't look so tragic! The secret of remaining young is never to have an emotion that is unbecoming. Come to the club with Basil and myself. We will smoke cigarettes and drink to the beauty of Sibyl Vane. She is beautiful. What more can you want?"

"Go away, Harry," cried the lad. "I want to be alone. Basil, you must go. Ah! Can't you see that my heart is breaking?" The hot tears came to his eyes. His lips trembled, and rushing to the back of the box, he leaned up against the wall, hiding his face in his hands.

"Let us go, Basil," said Lord Henry with a strange tenderness in his voice, and the two men passed out together.

A few moments afterward the footlights flared up and the curtain rose on the third act. Dorian Gray went back to his seat. He looked pale, and proud, and indifferent. The play dragged on. Half of the audience went out, tramping in heavy boots and laughing. The whole thing was a fiasco. The last act was played to almost empty benches. The curtain went down on a titter and some groans.

As soon as it was over, Dorian Gray rushed behind the scenes into the greenroom. The girl was standing there alone, with a look of triumph on her face. There was a radiance about her. Her parted lips were smiling over some secret of their own.

When he entered, she looked at him, and an expression of joy came over her. "How badly I acted tonight," she cried.

"Horribly!" he answered, gazing at her in amazement. "Horribly! It was dreadful. Are you ill? You have no idea what it was. You have no idea what I suffered."

The girl smiled. "Dorian," she answered, lingering over his name with long-drawn music in her voice, as though it were sweeter than honey to the red petals of her mouth. "Dorian, you should have understood. You understand now, don't you?"

"Understand what?" he asked, angrily.

"Why I was so bad tonight. Why I shall always be bad. Why I shall never act well again."

He shrugged his shoulders. "You are ill, I suppose. When you are ill you shouldn't act. You make yourself ridiculous. My friends were bored. I was bored."

She seemed not to listen to him. She was transfigured with joy. An ecstasy of happiness dominated her.

"Dorian, Dorian," she cried, "before I knew you, acting was the one reality of my life. It was only in the theater that I lived. I thought that it was all true. I was Rosalind one night and Portia the other. The joy of Beatrice was my joy, and the sorrows of Cordelia were mine also. I believed in everything. The common people who acted with me seemed to me to be godlike. The painted scenes were my world. I knew nothing but shadows, and I thought them real. You came – oh, my beautiful love! – and you freed my soul from prison. You taught me what reality really is. Tonight, for the first time in my life, I saw through the hollowness, the sham, the silliness of the empty pageant in which I had always played. Tonight, for the first time, I became conscious that the Romeo was hideous and old and painted, that the moonlight in the orchard was false, that the scenery was vulgar, and that the words I had to speak were unreal, were not my words, were not what I wanted to say. You had brought me something higher, something of which all art is but a reflection. You had made me understand what love really is. My love! My love! Prince Charming! Prince of life! I have grown sick of shadows. You are more to me than all art can ever be. What have I to do with the puppets of a play? When I came on tonight, I could not understand how it was that everything had gone from me. I thought that I was going to be wonderful. I found that I could do nothing. Suddenly it dawned on my soul what it all meant. The knowledge was exquisite to me. I heard them hissing, and I smiled. What could they know of love such as ours? Take me away, Dorian – take me away with you, where we can be quite alone. I hate the stage. I might mimic a passion that I do not feel, but I cannot mimic one that burns me like fire. Oh, Dorian, Dorian, you understand now what it signifies? Even if I could do it, it would be profanation for me to play at being in love. You have made me see that."

He flung himself down on the sofa and turned away his face. "You have killed my love," he muttered.

She looked at him in wonder and laughed. He made no answer. She came across to him, and with her little fingers stroked his hair. She knelt down and pressed his hands to her lips. He drew them away, and a shudder ran through him.

Then he leapt up and went to the door. "Yes," he cried, "you have killed my love. You used to stir my imagination.

Now you don't even stir my curiosity. You simply produce no effect. I loved you because you were marvelous, because you had genius and intellect, because you realized the dreams of great poets and gave shape and substance to the shadows of art. You have thrown it all away. You are shallow and stupid. My God! How

mad I was to love you! What a fool I have been! You are nothing to me now. I will never see you again. I will never think of you. I will never mention your name. You don't know what you were to me, once. Why, once . . . Oh, I can't bear to think of it! I wish I had never laid eyes upon you! You have spoiled the romance of my life. How little you can know of love, if you say it mars your art! Without your art, you are nothing. I would have made you famous, splendid, magnificent. The world would have worshipped you, and you would have borne my name. What are you now? A third-rate actress with a pretty face."

The girl grew white, and trembled. She clenched her hands together, and her voice seemed to catch in her throat. "You are not serious, Dorian?" she murmured. "You are acting."

"Acting! I leave that to you. You do it so well," he answered, and there was a heavy and now unmistakable bitterness in his voice.

She rose from her knees and, with a piteous expression of pain in her face, came across the room to him. She put her hand upon his arm and looked into his eyes. He thrust her back. "Don't touch me!" he cried.

A low moan broke from her, and she flung herself at his feet and lay there like a trampled flower. "Dorian, Dorian, don't leave me!" she whispered. "I am so sorry I didn't act well. I was thinking of you all the time. But I will try – indeed, I will try. It came so suddenly across me, my love for you. I think I should never have known it if you had not kissed me – if we had not kissed each other. Kiss me again, my love. Don't go away from me. I couldn't bear it. Oh! don't go away from me. My brother . . . No; never mind. He didn't mean it. He was in jest. . . . But you, oh! Can't you forgive me for tonight? I will work so hard and try to improve. Don't be cruel to me,

because I love you better than anything in the world. After all, it is only once that I have not pleased you. But you are quite right, Dorian. I should have shown myself more of an artist. It was foolish of me, and yet I couldn't help it. Oh, don't leave me, don't leave me." A fit of passionate sobbing choked her. She crouched on the floor like a wounded thing, and Dorian Gray, with his beautiful eyes, looked down at her, and his chiselled lips curled in exquisite disdain. There is always something ridiculous about the emotions of people whom one has ceased to love. Sibyl Vane seemed to him to be absurdly melodramatic. Her tears and sobs annoyed him.

"I am going," he said at last, in his calm, clear voice. "I don't wish to be unkind, but I can't see you again. You have disappointed me."

She wept silently, and made no answer, but crept nearer. Her little hands stretched blindly out, and appeared to be seeking for him. He turned on his heel and left the room. In a few moments he was out of the theater.

Where he went to he hardly knew. He remembered wandering through dimly lit streets, past gaunt, black-shadowed archways and evil-looking houses. Women with hoarse voices and harsh laughter had called after him. Drunkards had reeled by, cursing and chattering to themselves like monstrous apes. He had seen grotesque children huddled upon door steps, and heard shrieks and oaths from gloomy courts.

As the dawn was just breaking, he found himself close to Covent Garden. The darkness lifted, and, flushed with faint fires, the sky hollowed itself into a perfect pearl. Huge carts filled with nodding lilies rumbled slowly down the polished, empty street. The air was heavy with the perfume of the flowers, and their beauty seemed to soothe his pain. He followed into the market and watched the men unloading their wagons. A white-smocked carter offered him some cherries. He thanked him, wondered why he refused to accept any money for them, and began to eat them listlessly. They had been plucked at midnight, and the coldness of the moon had entered into them. A long line of boys carrying crates of striped tulips, and of yellow and red roses, filed in front of him, threading their way through the huge, jade-green piles of vegetables. Under the portico, with its gray, sun-bleached pillars, loitered a troop of draggled bare-headed girls, waiting for the auction to be over. Others crowded round the swinging doors of the coffee house in the piazza. The heavy cart-horses slipped and stamped upon the rough stones, shaking their bells and trappings. Some of the drivers were lying asleep on a pile of sacks. Iris-necked and pink-footed, the pigeons ran about picking up seeds.

After a little while, he hailed a hansom and drove home. For a few moments he loitered upon the doorstep, looking round at the silent square, with its blank, close-shuttered windows and its staring blinds. The sky was pure opal now, and the roofs of the houses glistened like silver against it. From some chimney opposite a thin wreath of smoke was rising. It curled, a violet riband, through the nacre-colored air.

In the huge gilt Venetian lantern, spoil of some Doge's barge, that hung from the ceiling of the great, oak-paneled hall of entrance, lights were still burning from three flickering jets: thin blue petals of flame they seemed, rimmed with white fire. He turned them out and, having thrown his hat and cape on the table, passed through the library toward the door of his bedroom, a large octagonal chamber on the ground floor that, in his newborn feeling for luxury, he had just had decorated for himself and hung with some curious Renaissance tapestries that had been discovered stored in a disused attic at Selby Royal. As he was turning the handle of the door, his eye fell upon the portrait Basil Hallward had painted of him. He started back as if in surprise. Then he went on into his own room, looking somewhat puzzled. After he had taken the button hole out of his coat, he seemed to hesitate. Finally, he came back, went over to the picture, and examined it. In the dim arrested light that struggled through the cream-colored silk blinds, the face appeared to him to be a little changed. The expression looked different. One would have said that there was a touch of cruelty in the mouth. It was certainly strange.

He turned round and, walking to the window, drew up the blind. The bright dawn flooded the room and swept the fantastic shadows into dusky corners, where they lay shuddering. But the strange expression that he had noticed in the face of the portrait seemed to linger there, to be more intensified even. The quivering, ardent sunlight showed him the lines of cruelty round the mouth as clearly as if he had been looking into a mirror after he had done some dreadful thing.

He winced and, taking up from the table an oval glass framed in ivory Cupids – one of Lord Henry's many presents to him – glanced hurriedly into its polished depths. No line like that warped his red lips. What did it mean?

He rubbed his eyes, and came close to the picture, and examined it again. There were no signs of any change when he looked into the actual painting, and yet there was no doubt that the whole expression had altered. It was not a mere fancy of his own. The thing was horribly apparent.

He threw himself into a chair and began to think. Suddenly there flashed across his mind what he had said in Basil Hallward's studio the day the picture had been finished. Yes, he remembered it perfectly. He had uttered a mad wish that he himself might remain young, and the portrait grow old; that his own beauty might be untarnished, and the face on the canvas bear the burden of his passions and his sins; that the painted image might be seared with the lines of suffering and thought, and that he might keep all the delicate bloom and loveliness of his then just conscious boyhood. Surely his wish had not been fulfilled? Such things were impossible. It seemed monstrous even to think of them. And, yet, there was the picture before him, with the touch of cruelty in the mouth that had not been there before.

Cruelty! Had he been cruel? It was the girl's fault, not his. He had dreamed of her as a great artist, had given his love to her because he had thought her great. Then she had disappointed him. She had been shallow and unworthy. And, yet, a feeling of infinite regret came over him, as he thought of her lying at his feet sobbing like a little child. He remembered with what callousness he had watched her. Why had he been made like that? Why had such a soul been given to him? But he had suffered also. During the three terrible hours that the play had lasted, he had lived centuries of pain, aeon upon aeon of torture. His life was well worth hers. She had marred him for a moment, if he had wounded her for an age. Besides, women were better suited to bear sorrow than men. They lived on their emotions. They only thought of their emotions. When they took lovers, it was merely to have someone with whom they could have scenes. Lord Henry had told him that, and Lord Henry knew what women were. Why should he trouble about Sibyl Vane? She was nothing to him now.

But the picture? What was he to say of that? It held the secret of his life, and told his story. It had taught him to love his own beauty. Would it teach him to loathe his own soul? Would he ever look at it again?

No; it was merely an illusion wrought on the troubled senses. The horrible night that he had passed had left phantoms behind it. Yet it was watching him, with its beautiful marred face and its cruel smile. Its bright hair gleamed in the early sunlight. Its blue eyes met his own. A sense of infinite pity, not for himself, but for the painted image of himself, came over him. It had altered already, and would alter more. Its gold would wither into gray. Its red and white roses would die. For every sin that he committed, a stain would fleck and wreck its fairness. But he would not sin again. The picture, changed or unchanged, would be to him the visible emblem of conscience. He would resist temptation. He would not see Lord Henry any more – would not, at any rate, listen to those subtle poisonous theories that in Basil Hallward's garden had first stirred within him the passion for impossible things. He would go back to Sibyl Vane, try to make her amends, marry her if she would have him, and try to love her again. Yes, it was his duty to do so. She must have suffered far more than he had. The poor child! He had been selfish and cruel to her. The fascination that she had once exercised over him would return.

He got up from his chair and drew a large screen right in front of the portrait, shuddering as he glanced at it. "How horrible!" he murmured to himself, and he walked across to the window and opened it.

When he stepped out onto the grass, he drew a long, deep breath. He could think only of Sibyl. A faint echo of his love had begun to come back to him. He repeated her name over and over again. The birds that were singing in the dew-drenched garden seemed to be telling the flowers about her.

It was long past noon when he awoke. His valet had crept several times on tiptoe into the room to see if he was stirring, and had wondered what made his young master sleep so late. Finally his bell sounded, and Victor came in softly with a cup of tea and a pile of letters on a small tray, and drew back the olive-satin curtains, with their shimmering blue lining, that hung in front of the three tall windows.

"Monsieur has slept well this morning," he said, smiling.

"What o'clock is it, Victor?" asked Dorian Gray drowsily.

"One hour and a quarter, monsieur."

How late it was! He sat up, and having sipped some tea, turned over his letters. One of them was from Lord Henry, and had been brought by hand that morning. He hesitated for a moment, and then put it aside. The others he opened listlessly. They contained the usual collection of cards, invitations to dinner, tickets for private views, programs of charity concerts, and the like that are showered on fashionable young men every morning during the season.

After about ten minutes he got up, and throwing on an elaborate dressing gown of silk-embroidered cashmere wool, passed into the onyx-paved bathroom. The cool water refreshed him after his long sleep. He seemed to have forgotten all that he had gone through. A dim sense of having taken part in some strange tragedy came to him once or twice, but there was the unreality of a dream about it.

As soon as he was dressed, he went into the library and sat down to a light French breakfast that had been laid out for him on a small round table close to the open window. It was an exquisite day. The warm air seemed laden with spices. A bee flew in and buzzed round the blue dragon bowl that, filled with roses, stood before him.

Suddenly his eye fell on the screen that he had placed in front of the portrait, and he started.

"Too cold for *monsieur*?" asked his valet, putting an omelet on the table. "I shut the window?"

Dorian shook his head. "I am not cold," he murmured.

Was it all true? Had the portrait really changed? Or had it been simply his own imagination that had made him see a look of evil where there had been a look of joy? The thing was absurd. It would serve as a tale to tell Basil some day. It would make him smile.

And, yet, how vivid was his recollection of the whole thing! First in the dim twilight, and then in the bright dawn, he had seen the touch of cruelty round the warped lips. He almost dreaded his valet leaving the room. He knew that when he was alone he would have to examine the portrait. He was afraid of certainty. As the door was closing behind him, he called him back. The man stood waiting for his orders. Dorian looked at him for a moment. "I am not at home to anyone, Victor," he said with a sigh. The man bowed and retired.

Then he rose from the table, lit a cigarette, and flung himself down on a luxuriously cushioned couch that stood facing the screen. The screen was an old one, of gilt Spanish leather, stamped and wrought with a rather florid Louis-Quatorze pattern. He scanned it curiously, wondering if ever before it had concealed the secret of a man's life.

Should he move it aside, after all? Why not let it stay there? What was the use of knowing? If the thing was true, it was terrible. If it was not true, why trouble about it? But what if, by some fate or deadlier chance, eyes other than his spied behind and saw the horrible change? What should he do if Basil Hallward came and asked to look at his own picture? Basil would be sure to do that. No; the thing had to be examined. Anything would be better than this dreadful state of doubt.

He got up and locked both doors. At least he would be alone when he looked upon the mask of his shame. Then he drew the screen aside and saw himself face to face. It was perfectly true, no one could deny the fact that the portrait had altered.

As he often remembered afterward, and always with no small wonder, he found himself at first gazing at the portrait with a feeling of almost scientific interest. That such a change should have taken place was incredible to him. And yet it was a fact. Was there some subtle affinity between the chemical atoms that shaped themselves into form and color on the canvas and the soul that was within him? Could it be that what that soul thought, they realized? That what it dreamed, they made true? Or was there some other, more terrible reason? He shuddered, and felt afraid, and, going back to the couch, lay there, gazing at the picture in sickened horror.

One thing, however, he felt that it had done for him. It had made him conscious how unjust, how cruel, he had been to Sibyl Vane. It was not too late to make reparation for that. She could still be his wife. His unreal and selfish love would yield to some higher influence, would be transformed into some nobler passion, and the portrait that Basil Hallward had painted of him would be a guide to him through life, would be to him what holiness is to some, and conscience to others. There were opiates for remorse, drugs that could lull the moral sense to sleep. But here was a visible symbol of the degradation of sin.

Three o'clock struck, and four, and the half-hour rang its double chime, but still Dorian Gray did not stir. He did not know what to do, or what to think. Finally, he went over to the table and wrote a passionate letter to the girl he had loved, imploring her forgiveness and accusing himself of madness. He covered page after page with wild words of sorrow and wilder words of pain. There is a luxury in self-reproach. When we blame ourselves, we feel that no one else has a right to blame us. It is the confession, not the priest, that gives us absolution. When Dorian had finished the letter, he felt comforted and that he had been forgiven.

Suddenly there came a knock to the door, and he heard Lord Henry's voice outside. "My dear boy, I must see you."

He made no answer at first. The knocking still continued. Yes, it was better to let Lord Henry in, and to explain to him the new life he was going to lead. He would be firm and not listen to his friend's talk, he would explain his new plan to him and make him understand. Dorian jumped up, drew the screen across the picture, and unlocked the door.

"I am so sorry for it all, Dorian," said Lord Henry as he entered. "But you must not think too much about it."

"Do you mean about Sibyl Vane?" asked the lad.

"Yes, of course," answered Lord Henry, sinking into a chair, "It is dreadful, from one point of view, but it was not your fault. Did you go behind and see her, after the play was over?"

"Yes."

"I felt sure you had. Did you make a scene with her?"

"I was brutal. But it is all right now. I am not sorry for anything that has happened. It has taught me to know better."

"Ah, Dorian, I am so glad you take it in that way!"

"I am perfectly happy now." Said Dorian, "I know what conscience is, to begin with. It is not what you told me it was. It is the divinest thing in us. Don't sneer Harry, I want to be good. I can't bear the idea of my soul being hideous."

"A very charming artistic basis for ethics, Dorian! I congratulate you on it. But how are you going to begin?"

"By marrying Sibyl Vane."

"Marrying Sibyl Vane!" cried Lord Henry, standing up and looking at him in perplexed amazement. "But, my dear Dorian—"

"Yes, Henry, I know what you are going to say. Something dreadful about marriage. I am not going to break my word. She is to be my wife."

"Your wife! Dorian! Didn't you get my letter?"

"Your letter? Oh, yes, I have not read it yet, Henry. I was afraid there might be something in it that I wouldn't like. It is over there if you wish to read it to me now."

"You know nothing then?"

"What do you mean?"

Lord Henry walked across the room, and sitting down by Dorian Gray, took both his hands in his own and held them tightly. "Dorian," he said, "my letter – don't be frightened – was to tell you that Sibyl Vane is dead."

GHOSTS THAT HAVE HAUNTED ME

J. K. Bangs

It happened last Christmas, in my own home. I had provided as a little surprise for my wife a complete new solid silver service marked with her initials. The tree had been prepared for the children, and all had retired save myself. I had lingered later than the others to put the silver service under the tree, where its happy recipient would find it when she went to the tree with the little ones the next morning. It made a magnificent display: the two dozen of each kind of spoon, the forks, the knives, the coffee pot, water urn, and all; the salvers, the vegetable dishes, olive forks, cheese scoops, and other dazzling attributes of a complete service, not to go into details, presented a fairly scintillating picture which would have made me gasp if I had not, at the moment when my own

breath began to catch, heard another
gasp in the corner immediately behind me.
Turning about quickly to see whence it came,
I observed a dark figure in the pale light of the
moon which streamed in through the window.

"Who are you?" I cried, starting back, the
physical symptoms of a ghostly presence
manifesting themselves as usual.

"I am the ghost of one long gone before,"
was the reply, in sepulchral tones.

I breathed a sigh of relief, for I had for a moment
feared it was a burglar.

"Oh!" I said. "You gave me a
start at first. I was afraid you were
a material thing come to rob me."
Then turning toward the tree,
I observed, with a wave of
the hand, "Fine layout, eh?"

"Beautiful," he said, hollowly.
"Yet not so beautiful as things
I've seen in realms beyond
your ken."

And then he set about
telling me of the beautiful
gold and silverware
they used in the
Elysian Fields, and I must
confess Monte Cristo would

99

have had a hard time, with Sinbad the Sailor to help, to surpass the picture of royal magnificence the specter drew. I stood enthralled until, even as he was talking, the clock struck three, when he rose up, and moving slowly across the floor, barely visible, murmured regretfully that he must be off, with which he faded away down the back stairs. I pulled my nerves, which were getting rather strained, together again, and went to bed.

Next morning, every bit of that silverware was gone; and, what is more, three weeks later I found the ghost's picture in the Rogue's Gallery in New York as that of the cleverest sneak thief in the country.

All of which, let me say to you, dear reader, in conclusion, proves that when you are dealing with ghosts you mustn't give up all your physical resources until you have definitely ascertained that the thing by which you are confronted, horrid or otherwise, is a ghost, and not an all too material rogue with a light step, and a commodious jute bag for plunder concealed beneath his coat.

"How to tell a ghost?" you ask.

Well, as an eminent master of fiction frequently observes in his writings, "that is another story," which I shall hope some day to tell for your instruction and my own aggrandizement.

J. K. Bangs

1862 – 1922

United States (Yonkers, New York)

While most ghost story writers aim to shock and thrill their readers, most also mean to scare them – sending shivers of fear down their spines. But not John Kendrick Bangs! He wants to shock and thrill you with laughter.

The author and satirist was born in Yonkers, New York, to a father who was a lawyer. Like many sons of lawyers, Bangs attempted to follow in his father's footsteps. He studied at Columbia University from 1880 to 1883 and became editor of Columbia's literary magazine. During this time, he submitted short, anonymous pieces to humor magazines. This most likely whetted his appetite for the written word. After his first year of law school, Bangs left to become associate editor of *Life* magazine in 1884.

During his time at *Life*, from 1884 to 1888, Bangs wrote articles and poems for the magazine. He also wrote and published his first books, *A House-Boat on the Styx* (1895) and *Pursuit of the House-Boat* (1897). Styx is the mythological river of the underworld that serves as the passageway from the land of the living to the land of the dead. If it strikes you as funny to think of a houseboat on such a river, you're not alone. Bangs was famous for writing stories that set the plot wholly or partially in the afterlife. His writing was so popular

103

for the humorous afterlife element, in fact, that he developed a whole school of storytelling that became known as the Bangsian fantasy.

While writing ghost stories for readers with a funny bone, Bangs held a day job in editorial work. In 1888, Bangs left *Life* (the magazine, not the land of the living, though that would be fitting) to work at *Harper's Magazine, Harper's Bazaar,* and *Harper's Young People*. He was the humor department editor for all three magazines until 1900. He also served as editor of *Harper's Weekly* from 1889 to 1901 and briefly served as the first editor of *Munsey's Magazine* (1889) and the Harper-owned publication *Literature* (1899).

He finished his career with *Harper's* in 1901 and went on to edit *New Metropolitan* magazine in 1903. His last magazine was *Puck* (1904), which was one of the top humor magazines of its day. Among all of his editorial work, Bangs still had time to write fiction. He published *The Enchanted Type-Writer* in 1899, and in 1901, he produced *Mr. Munchausen: Being a True Account of Some of the Recent Adventures Beyond the Styx of the Late Hieronymus Carl Friedrich, Sometime Baron Munchausen of Bodenwerder, as Originally Reported for the Sunday Edition of the Gehenna Gazette by its Special Interviewer the Late Mr. Ananias Formerly of Jerusalem and Now First Transcribed from the Columns of that Journal.*

In 1906, Bangs switched from writing to giving lectures.

Sir Arthur Conan Doyle

1859 – 1930

Scotland

Sir Arthur Conan Doyle was a doctor, Spiritualist, and writer best known for his Sherlock Holmes detective thrillers. *The Hound of the Baskervilles* is rooted in British folklore. When the story was first published in *The Strand* in 1901, the magazine went into seven printings for the only time in its history. By 1920, Conan Doyle was one of the most highly paid writers in the world.

Born in Edinburgh, Scotland, Conan Doyle was surrounded by a family of artists. His mother's storytelling techniques included lowering her voice to a terrifying whisper at the most significant moments. His father was a painter, book illustrator, and sketch artist for criminal trials. His uncle was an illustrator and his grandfather was a caricaturist. In rebellion against his artistic family, Conan Doyle pursued a medical career before committing to a life of full-time writing.

After studying medicine at Edinburgh University, where he met other future authors Robert Louis Stevenson and James Barrie, Conan Doyle opened a medical practice. He saw few patients and spent his free time crafting stories with a central character based on a teacher who was a master at observation, logic, deduction, and diagnosis. The character he developed later became known as the world famous Dr. Sherlock Holmes.

Conan Doyle was frustrated with his development of Holmes and, on several occasions, attempted to kill him off so that he could work on more "literary" pursuits. In reaction to the first death of Holmes, twenty thousand Conan Doyle fans cancelled their subscriptions to *The Strand*.

His next novel was based on a visit to the Devonshire moors and Dartmoor Prison. He resurrected his old friend, Sherlock Holmes, for *The Hound of the Baskervilles*, framing the story as a previously untold adventure.

Throughout his career, he developed another character that was almost the opposite of Holmes: Professor Challenger, the hero of *The Lost World* (1912). The series serves as the platform for much modern-day Science Fiction.

Toward the later part of his career, Conan Doyle became increasingly interested in Spiritualism, a popular belief in the early twentieth century that suggested people could communicate with beings in the spiritual realm, such as ghosts and fairies. Conan Doyle's commitment to his Spiritualist beliefs appears in his later writings, such as *The Coming of the Fairies* (1921), the Professor Challenger novel, *The Land of Mist* (1926), and a piece about his friend, the magician Harry Houdini, *The Edge of the Unknown* (1930).

After a long career of storytelling, Sir Arthur Conan Doyle died of heart disease in his home in England at the age of 71.

J. Sheridan Le Fanu
1814 – 1873
Ireland

Joseph Thomas Sheridan Le Fanu started writing supernatural stories as a young man. He was a bestselling author in his day for works such as the vampire story *Carmilla* (1871-1872) and a short story collection *In a Glass Darkly* (1872). During the Victorian era, it was the custom, according to author Henry James, for hosts to place a volume of Le Fanu's stories on a guest's bedside table for "the hours after midnight." Although Le Fanu is considered a forerunner of modern horror fiction and was widely read during his day, it remains a mystery that he is widely forgotten today.

The "father of the modern ghost story," Le Fanu was born in Dublin. His father was a clergyman, his grandmother and great-uncle were both playwrights, and his niece became a novelist. Le Fanu began writing poems at an early age. He then went on to study law at Trinity College, but after passing the Irish Bar, he never practiced law. Instead, he worked as a journalist. His first story, "The Ghost and the Bone-Setter" was published in 1938 in the *Dublin University Magazine*. Over the years, several of his stories were published in the magazine and were later collected in *The Purcell Papers* (1880).

In 1837, Le Fanu joined the staff of *Dublin University Magazine*, and, in 1861, he became owner and editor of the magazine.

During his time at the magazine, he published the novel *The Clock and Anchor* (1845) and a collection, *Ghost Stories and Tales of Mystery* (1851). He also owned or part-owned several Dublin newspapers through his life. His best-known work is the suspense novel, *Uncle Silas* (1864).

After the death of his wife, Le Fanu became depressed and worked his dark thoughts into stories. He was nicknamed "The Invisible Prince" due to his reclusive nature, shyness, and nocturnal lifestyle, and his son reported that his father often wrote from midnight to dawn by candlelight.

Le Fanu's stories often involved strange events filled with suspense. His plots were vivid, and he specialized in tone and effect delivered through mystery, rather than shock. He focused on the inner, psychological effects of terror rather than the external elements that sparked fear.

The influence of *Carmilla* was far-reaching, and the novel served as inspiration for Bram Stoker's *Dracula*. Le Fanu's early work *A Chapter in the History of the Tyrone Family* (1839) is said to have influenced Emily Brontë's *Wuthering Heights*.

After Le Fanu's death, ghost story writer M. R. James (*The Haunted Doll's House*) published a collection of Le Fanu's stories titled *Madam Crow's Ghost and Other Tales of Mystery* (1923).

E. Nesbit

1858 – 1924

England

Edith Nesbit wrote more than sixty books during her lifetime, mostly fiction for children, and published under the gender-neutral names E. Nesbit and Fabian Bland. She is best known for her three books in the *Treasure Seekers* (1899-1904) series. With her husband, Hubert Bland, she also helped found the Fabian Society, which consisted of a group of freethinkers who promoted social change in London.

Edith Nesbit was born in Kennington, Surrey, which is now part of Greater London. Her father was a schoolteacher who died before Nesbit's fourth birthday. Because of her sister's ill health, the family moved throughout continental Europe during her childhood. She was somewhat a tomboy as a child, and her family's home in Kent served as inspiration for *The Railway Children* (1906).

At the age of twenty-two, Nesbit married a bank clerk, Hubert Bland. Together, they kept an unconventional household. For the first part of their marriage, Bland continued to live with his mother. Later, when the couple finally did live together, Bland's girlfriend Alice Hoatson moved in with them. The three adults raised Nesbit, Bland, and Hoatson's children together. They also held meetings for socialist and literary discussion in their home.

Edith Nesbit was noted for her style and flair, being a tall woman adorned in gowns of peacock blue, strings of beads, and wrist bangles. Her fashion was to wear looser, less restrictive clothing than Victorian styles dictated.

Nesbit's writing reveals a keen sense for the world as children saw it. She reveled in her girlhood fantasies and told her stories in a manner that children could relate to. She was adept at combining real-life situations with elements of fantasy, magical objects, and humor. All of these elements appear in her widely anthologized story, "Man Size in Marble" (1893), and her popular novels *The Wouldbegoods* (1899), *The Five Children and It* (1902), *The Amulet* (1906), and *The Enchanted Castle* (1907).

Credited for inventing the children's adventure story, Nesbit inspired writers from P. L. Travers (*Mary Poppins*) and Rudyard Kipling (*The Jungle Book*) to C. S. Lewis (*The Chronicles of Narnia* series) and J. K. Rowling (*Harry Potter* series).

Fitz-James O'Brien
1828 – 1862
Ireland

Fitz-James O'Brien was one of the first writers to introduce an invisible creature as a source of horror with his story "What Was It? A Mystery" (1859). He is best known for his collections of stories that border on science fiction. Little is known about his childhood in Ireland, but after his 1852 arrival in Washington, D.C., he soon became well known among the Bohemian culture of New York City.

Born in County Limerick, Ireland, Fitz-James O'Brien was an only child. His father died when O'Brien was twelve years old, leaving behind a large sum of money. O'Brien went on to Trinity College in Dublin, to study a variety of topics, then to London in 1849. During his two and a half years in London, O'Brien managed to spend his entire inheritance, but he also published a large number of poems, stories, and articles. He also learned about the theater, which helped his later roles as playwright and critic.

O'Brien went to the United States in 1852, first arriving in Washington, D.C. He then moved to New York to live in the epicenter of the country's literary world, befriending other writers, such as Walt Whitman. Although he lived extravagantly, he also lived recklessly, which affected his work ethic. He often waited until his deadlines nipped at his heels before putting pen to paper.

O'Brien was, however, prolific in his writings, producing numerous poems, stories, humor pieces, sketches, columns, and reviews. He was a frequent contributor to the *Times*, *The American Whig Review*, *Harper's New Monthly Magazine and Weekly*, *Putnam's*, the *Atlantic Monthly*, *Vanity Fair*, the *Evening Post*, *Saturday Press*, the *Saturday Review*, and the comic journal the *Lantern*. His most notable play was *The Gentleman from Ireland* (1854). He also wrote a number of fantasies and ghost stories, such as "The Pot of Tulips" (1855).

The premier issue of the *Atlantic Monthly* featured his story "The Diamond Lens" (1858). O'Brien is said to have influenced Ambrose Bierce ("A Bottomless Grave"), in addition to other writers, with some of his groundbreaking imaginative themes, such as miniature people and animated manikins inhabited by evil spirits. His fantasy *From Hand to Mouth* was serialized in *The New York Picayune* in 1858 and was noted by Sam Moskowitz as "the single most striking example of surrealistic fiction to pre-date *Alice in Wonderland*."

Sparked by a dedication to his newfound homeland, O'Brien volunteered his adept skills in combat to the Union Army during the Civil War. His Civil War poems are considered to be among the best written. In his second battle, O'Brien was wounded in the shoulder. Due to inadequate medical attention, he died a few days later at the age of thirty-three. His legacy lives on, as he helped shape the medium of the short story at a time when it reached large audiences.

Edgar Allan Poe
1809 – 1849
United States (Boston, Massachusetts)

A master of the macabre short story, Poe lived a life of poverty, scandal, and ill health. He wrote poetry and worked as a journalist before becoming one of America's greatest-ever horror writers. His support of the short story as an art form transformed it. Once considered a vulgar form of writing, the short story rose to prominence under Poe's care. Today, Poe is credited with inventing gothic fiction and spearheading detective and crime fiction.

Edgar Allan Poe's parents were traveling actors who both died before he was two years old. Wealthy merchant John Allan took Poe in and raised him in Richmond, Virginia. During school in England and the United States, Poe's teachers recognized that his poetic gift distinguished him from his peers.

Poe attended the University of Virginia in 1826. He was expelled after building up a large gambling debt. John Allan then cut off all financial support, leaving Poe to struggle for funds. In 1827, Poe published his first volume of poetry, *Tamerlane*, which sold poorly. In 1829, Poe published a second book of poems, *Al Aaraaf, Tamerlane and Minor Poems*. He then attended West Point Academy. His fellow cadets collected funds for Poe to publish his third volume of poems, called *Poems by Edgar Allan Poe, Second Edition* (1831).

Baltimore became Poe's next home when he moved in with his widowed aunt and her daughter, Virginia, whom he married in 1836. He worked for various magazines after winning a prize for his short story, "MS Found in a Bottle." He became editor of the *Southern Literary Messenger* for two years and wrote numerous literary critiques that made him famous. He also edited *Burton's Gentleman's Magazine* and *Graham's Magazine*. Virginia died of tuberculosis in 1845. Poe responded to his sorrow by drinking heavily, which weakened his health.

His longest work was *The Narrative of Arthur Gordon Pym* (1838). The influence of his detective story, *The Murders in the Rue Morgue* (1841) can be seen in Sir Arthur Conan Doyle's Sherlock Holmes stories. Poe told stories to achieve a singular effect, such as fear in "The Fall of the House of Usher" (1839) and guilt in "The Tell-Tale Heart" (1843). His musical lyricism is evident in his poems "The Raven" (1845) and "The Bells" (1849). In his supernatural fiction, Poe focused on paranoia, obsessions, and damnation, rather than on ghosts, werewolves, or vampires.

The greatest mystery of Poe's life is in his death. He was found lying in a Baltimore street, incoherent and in poor health. A few days later, Edgar Allan Poe died.

Poe's memory still lives on today through his fans, his many writings, the influence of his works, and in the films that have been made of his chilling tales.

Bram Stoker

1847 – 1912

Ireland

Abraham "Bram" Stoker was born and educated in Dublin, Ireland, before becoming manager of London's Lyceum Theater. A pillar of respectable Victorian society, he spent his spare moments writing supernatural short stories and novels, including the worldwide bestseller *Dracula* (1897).

Bram Stoker spent the first seven years of life confined to bed, due to a recurring and undiagnosed childhood illness. The helplessness he experienced while bedridden no doubt made an impression on Stoker, and his later fiction tended to explore the themes of everlasting sleep and the resurrection of the dead.

Upon Stoker's recovery, he became a notable athlete at the University of Dublin. He also studied history, literature, math, and physics at the Trinity College.

Although Stoker had literary aspirations, he became a civil servant for eight years and worked as a freelance journalist and drama critic for *The Evening Mail*. While reviewing Henry Irving's performance in *Hamlet*, Stoker met the actor. Irving offered Stoker the position as manager at his Lyceum Theater. He accepted the position, moved to London in 1878, and served as Irving's manager for the next twenty-seven years.

Stoker married Florence Balcome, who had once been a girlfriend of Oscar Wilde ("The Canterville Ghost" and *The Picture of Dorian Gray*), and befriended such figures as Sir Arthur Conan Doyle (*The Hound of the Baskervilles* and creator of detective Sherlock Holmes). Stoker also devoted his free time to writing fiction. The London Society published his first story, "The Crystal Cup," in 1872. Ten years later, he published his first book, *Under the Sunset*, which was a collection of eight eerie fairy tales for children.

In 1890, Stoker published his first full-length novel, *The Snake's Pass*. That same year, he began researching vampires, a project that took seven years and became the definitive work of his career: *Dracula* (1897). Although Stoker published thirteen novels, no other work of his received as much critical acclaim, success, and worldwide fame as his vampire novel, which saw countless versions in film and on stage. For *Dracula*, Stoker used the epistolary format, which alternates among multiple narrators that tell the story through journals, diaries, letters, and newspaper articles.

Today, Stoker's name is inextricably linked with that of the character he created. Some scholars argue that, like Mary Shelley (*Frankenstein*, 1818), Stoker created a character that took on a life of its own and left the author nearly forgotten. Evidence of *Dracula*'s wild popularity and legendary status can be seen in the many vampire stories that have come afterward, leaving *Dracula* truly un-dead.

Oscar Wilde
1854 – 1900
Ireland

Oscar Fingal O'Flahertie Wilde's life is nearly as fascinating to scholars as the lives of the characters he created. He was an Irish writer who composed poetry, plays, short stories, and just one novel, *The Picture of Dorian Gray* (1891). He wrote of the characters in his novel, "Basil Hallward is what I think I am: Lord Henry what the world thinks of me: Dorian what I would like to be – in other ages, perhaps." This supernatural tale so unsettled and shocked readers that it caused a scandal when it was first printed in *Lippincott's Magazine* in 1890. But it was his publicly flamboyant, quippish nature that led to a larger scandal that overshadowed Wilde's later years and led to his penniless, secluded death in Paris. To this day, he is one of the most highly quoted literary figures for his witticisms.

Born in Dublin, Oscar Wilde was the son of a prominent surgeon and well-known journalist. Wilde's father, Sir William, was an antiquarian, archaeologist, folklorist, and specialist in ear and eye diseases. Wilde's mother was an Irish nationalist who wrote revolutionary poems under the name Speranza. Her translation of Wilhelm Meinhold's gothic horror novel, *Sidonia the Sorceress*, inspired Wilde to draw on its darker elements for his own work. Wilde's mother also held a regular Sunday discussion group that included as guest J. Sheridan Le Fanu (*Carmilla* and "Narrative of a Ghost Hand").

During Wilde's school years, he became acquainted with the Aesthetic Movement. He later became a notorious figure in his exaltation of this philosophy that advocated "art for art's sake," and he wore his hair long, donned colorful clothing, and had a habit of carrying flowers to his lectures.

In 1884, Wilde married Constance Lloyd. Together, they had two sons. With a family to support, Wilde worked for *Woman's World* magazine from 1887 to 1889. The next six years were the most creative of his career. During this time, he published two collections of children's stories, *The Happy Prince and Other Tales* (1888) and *The House of Pomegranates* (1892). Among several essays and poems and the novel *The Portrait of Dorian Gray* (1891), he also wrote four wildly popular plays: *Lady Windermere's Fan* (1892), *A Woman of No Importance* (1893), *An Ideal Husband* (1895), and *The Importance of Being Earnest* (1895).

Wilde's singular novel, *The Portrait of Dorian Gray*, served as a key piece of evidence in his famous Queensbury trial, where he was convicted of "gross indecency with other male persons" and sentenced to serve two years of hard labor. His health never recovered from his time in prison, and he spent the next three years in hiding under an assumed name. He died at the age of 46 from cerebral meningitis.

Just a month before his death, Wilde is quoted as saying, "My wallpaper and I are fighting a duel to the death. One or the other of us has got to go."

GHASTLY GLOSSARY

absolution—the act of setting free the guilt from sins

accordance—agreement

actuated—moved into action

aeon—an indefinitely long period of time

aggrandizement—to make something seem great

agile—having the ability to move quickly, with ease and grace

agitated—disturbed or moved in an irregular, vigorous manner

alighting—coming down from the air and landing on a surface

amalgamation—the act or result of uniting or merging

appalls—horrifies; frightens; disgusts; overcomes with dismay

apparition—the appearance of an unexpected sight

arabesque—an elaborate, sometimes floral pattern

Arcadian—simple, pastoral, quiet, or untroubled

ardent—characterized by warmth

ascertained—learned with certainty

assailant—a person (or other creature) who attacks violently

august—marked by majesty, elegance, dignity, and grandness

Avatar—the embodiment of a concept

bier balk—the frame where a coffin is placed for carrying

boyars—members of the Russian aristocratic order

cadaverous—of or relating to a dead body

casements—window coverings

ceased—stopped; brought to an end

cessation—the stopping of an activity

chancel—the part of a church that contains the altar and seats for the clergy and choir

commenced—began; started an activity

commodious—roomy, spacious

conceptions—ideas, the having of ideas, or the concrete results or manifestations of ideas

conformation—the forming of something or arranging of parts to assemble into a whole; the shape of a plan

confounded—confused, perplexed, or doomed

conscience—the sense or awareness of moral goodness

constrained—confined, limited, held back by force

contagion—a disease-producing agent

convulsed—shook violently and/or irregularly

coppices—thickets or groves of small trees

corporeal—of or relating to the body or the physical world

corridor—passageway or hallway

countenance—the face, or the look or expression on the face, often revealing mood

courtiers—those who attend the royal court

credulity—the willingness to believe

daunted—deflated courage

dauntless—fearless

delirious—confused; suffering from frenzied excitement or a loss of senses

despairing—entirely losing hope

diabolical—of or relating to the devil; devilish

diligence—stagecoach

disapprobation—disapproval; the act of rejecting

discontinuance—interruption; the act of stopping

disposed—inclined; given to a tendency

divinest—closest to God or a god; most heavenly or supreme

dominion—a territory; ruling or having authority over a region

effigies—figures or images representing certain people

egress—exit

elocution—the art of public speaking

eloquence—exhibiting fluid and persuasive speech

emanating—coming out of a source

embellishments—decorations, ornamentations

enigma—a mystery; something that is hard to understand or hard to explain

entreaties—pleas; urgent requests similar to begging

facsimile—a copy

faugh—an expression used to express contempt or disgust

fête—a festival or elaborate party

flange—a rim for strength, guiding, or attaching to another object

florid—covered with flowers or flowery in style

gait—a manner of walking or moving on foot

gesticulating—making gestures or hand movements

gilt—covered with a thin coat of gold

gouts—masses of fluid bursting forth

grotesque—fanciful, bizarre, an absurd distortion of nature

hackles—the hairs along the neck and back

hansom—a light, two-wheeled, covered carriage

hearken—to listen or give respectful attention to

hideous—ugly, shocking, or offensive to the senses

homogeneous—of a uniform structure; all parts are the same

humility—the quality or state of being humble

illimitable—measureless; without limits

illumined—lit up; brightened with a light

imperial—regal

impotently—without power or strength

improvisatori—those who improvise; people who perform on the spot, making use of the material that is on hand

imputation—the act of blaming, often a wrongful accusation

inanimate—not alive

incredulity—unbelievability

incredulous—the unwillingness to believe

induced—stimulated, caused, influenced, moved
by persuasion

inert—lacking the power to move

ingress—entrance

insensible—lacking in sense; foolish

instigation—the act of urging to move forward

ken—sight; view; range of knowing or perception

lineaments—outlines or features that distinguish an object

lintels—horizontal structures that support the weight above
an opening

ludicrous—amusing or laughable

malice—desire or intent to cause pain, distress, or harm
to another

manacled—handcuffed or shackled around the wrists

manifest—to appear or make evident by visibly showing

marauders—those who roam around and raid in search
of riches

marred—spoiled, injured, flawed, or blemished

masquerade—a social gathering of people wearing costumes

mediocre—ordinary; of moderate or low quality

meerschaum—a tobacco pipe

melodramatic—overly emotional or sensational

metaphysical—abstract; supernatural; not in the physical world

monotonous—repetitive; lacking in variation

moor—a boggy area of land

mummer—performer, actor

nacre—mother-of-pearl

obtruding—thrusting out; imposing

occult—hidden from view; supernatural

opiates—drugs containing opium and tending to cause
sleep and alleviate pain

overemphasized—stressed, or emphasized, more
than necessary

pageant—a dramatic show

paradox—a seeming contradiction

perceive—to gain understanding through the senses

perfidious—characterized by faithlessness

perforce—by force or physical coercion

pestilence—a contagious epidemic disease that is destructive

phantasms—illusions or ghosts

phantoms—ghosts

phenomena—objects known through the senses rather
than thoughts

physiognomy—outward appearance of internal
characteristics

picturesque—resembling a picture; charming; evoking
mental images

pinioned—restrained by binding the arms

piteous—one that exhibits a quality that would move another to sympathetic sorrow

placid—calm; free of disturbance

ponderous—heavy, cumbersome, or unwieldy and clumsy due to weight and size

precincts—territories; limits or boundaries

precipice—a very steep or overhanging place; brink or edge

presentiments—feelings that something is about to happen

profanation—the act of desecrating or treating with disrespect

profuse—bountiful; extravagant

pulsations—rhythmical throbs that indicate the beating of the heart

purport—meaning

reiteration—wearisome repetition

rejoined—replied sharply and quickly

repose—peaceful rest

repugnance—disgust; strong dislike

reticulated—marked by crossing lines; resembling a net

revel—to take intense pleasure; party, celebration

reverie—the condition of being lost in thought

riband—a ribbon used for decoration

rogue—a dishonest or worthless person; scoundrel

sagacious—wise; having good judgment or perception

salvers—trays of food

scintillating—brilliantly lively or stimulating

scourge—cause of affliction, pain, or grief

sepulchral—having the characteristics of a burial tomb

serrated—notched along the edge

shambling—shuffling; walking awkwardly with dragging feet

sinewy—stringy, showing stretched tendons through the skin

solemn—marked by seriousness and reverence

spectral—ghostly

stile—a step or set of steps for getting over a fence

succumb—to yield to superior strength

supposition—something that is believed, imagined, formulated, or understood

surmounted—topped off; attached above

tangible—capable of being touched or perceived by the senses

teeming—overflowing

throng—crowd; a multitude of assembled parts or a large number

transfigured—changed; given a new appearance for the good

treacherous—marked by hidden dangers

tremulous—characterized by trembling; timid nervousness

uncanniness—weirdness, eeriness, mysteriousness

unfeigned—genuine, sincere

untenanted—not lived in

vengeance—revenge, retribution

verification—the act or process of confirming or establishing the truth, accuracy, or reality of

vesta—a short, wooden match

vesture—a robe or covering garment

vexed—troubled, disturbed, confused

vulgar—ordinary; coarse, common, or uncultivated

writhe—wind, intertwine, twist

wrought—worked into shape by artistry or effort